ETHNIC AMERICANS
A History of
Immigration and Assimilation

IRWIN UNGER
NEW YORK UNIVERSITY
Consulting Editor

Ethnic Americans

A HISTORY OF IMMIGRATION AND ASSIMILATION

Leonard Dinnerstein

UNIVERSITY OF ARIZONA

David M. Reimers

NEW YORK UNIVERSITY

Dodd, Mead & Company

NEW YORK   1975

To:
Rachel, Anahid, and Natalie Kabasakalian,
and
Jack and Marjorie Reimers

Contents

List of Tables

Editor's Introduction

There was a time, soon after World War II, when Americans assumed that their "nation of nations" had finally become one. The end of free immigration during the 1920s and the shared experiences of the Depression and of the War, seemed to have finally fused all the ethnic elements into a uniform blend. Still unmerged were nonwhites, particularly blacks, but in the 1950s even they appeared likely to eventually coalesce into the new mixture that made up the American people.

But this was a mistaken assumption. Blacks, of course, did not lose their separate identity. In fact the events of the 1960s gave them, if anything, a stronger sense of their distinctiveness and their apartness from the rest of America. More to the point here, Americans learned how strong were the emotional ties that these "ethnics" had to their cultural past and to their origins and group identity. Partly in emulation of, partly in reaction to, the new mood of black self-consciousness, Italian Americans, Hispanic Americans, Greek Americans, Polish Americans, and many other varieties of what used to be called "hyphenated" Americans, began to assert their right to cultivate and retain their unique cultural, historical, and even political identities.

It is this growing interest in "ethnicity" that has inspired this volume by Professors Dinnerstein and Reimers. The book emphasizes the successive waves of new arrivals on American shores from the 1840s onward. It examines the circumstances of their departure from their original homelands and describes their reception in America. It includes an unusually full treatment of the post 1920s arrivals, including the war refugees of the 1935–60 period, and the mass movement of Hispanic peoples—Puerto Ricans,

Mexicans, Cubans, and other Latin Americans—to the United States after 1945.

Unlike many of the works on immigration, this book does not stop with the immigrants safely ashore at Ellis Island. It also deals with their difficult problems of adjusting to an alien environment. Still more unusual, it continues the story of ethnic adjustment to the second and third generations. We learn from it much about the difficulties faced by immigrants, their children, and even their grandchildren, in dealing with the complex and often harsh environment of the United States. The book has an entire chapter on assimilation and one on social and economic mobility.

The Dinnerstein–Reimers work is geared to the growing awareness in our own day that the "melting-pot," so proudly proclaimed by liberals earlier in the century, has really not worked out. This is the first study, I believe, that has recognized this as a major premise and has successfully fitted the great social phenomenon of mass migration to America into such a modern and relevant framework.

IRWIN UNGER

Preface

Eᴛʜɴɪᴄ Aᴍᴇʀɪᴄᴀɴs is the history primarily of non-English American immigration and assimilation. Our focus is on those people who came voluntarily to the New World after 1607. By limiting the topic in this fashion we have obviously not included American Indians and blacks. Their history is in many respects unique and requires separate treatment.

In a book of this length we had to make many choices. Over 46 million people came to America in the past 350 years, and no account of this number can cover all groups and events. First, we have stressed the modern era, that is, America since the 1840s. We have given some attention to the period before the 1840s but only as a necessary background to the main story.

Second, we have emphasized certain developments and groups at the expense of others. But even though we have concentrated on the non-English minorities, we have also given some attention to immigration from Great Britain, which is necessary to understand the cultural foundations of America and nativism. Among the immigrant minorities large groups are obviously more important than small groups, but numbers alone have not been our criteria. Some ethnic groups* have been small in numbers, but their experience in America has been especially illustrative of broader themes and developments; hence we have singled out these groups to a greater extent than their numbers might warrant. The historical and sociological literature focuses more on some groups, and because this is a short survey we have drawn upon the more abundant materials for our narrative.

* We use ethnic group to mean a group with a shared culture and sense of identity based on religion, race, or nationality.

The reader will find that we have not emphasized the "contributions" of this or that group to American life; nor will he find that
we have discussed the roles of particular ethnic individuals in the
numerous wars in which Americans have been engaged. It has
never been demonstrated that members of one ethnic group are
braver or more patriotic than members of any other ethnic group.
Nor will we recite facts, achievements, and names to show that a
particular group should be proud of its heritage. We assume that
all ethnic groups have enriched American life, and we are not
trying to bolster ethnic egos. Rather, we have stressed the broad
themes of ethnic history, the problems of the newcomers, their
struggles and conflicts, patterns of mobility and assimilation in order
to get at the meaning of the immigrant and ethnic experience.

The reader will quickly recognize that all groups had some
common experiences. Practically all suffered to some degree in the
New World. They struggled to advance economically and to win
friends; they experienced generational conflicts and alienation; and
they met with native hostility. Older generations of Americans
were often suspicious of newcomers and did not want foreign enclaves in their midst. Germans in the colonial era who saw no need
to learn English aroused the same scorn as have Mexicans with a
similar outlook today.

For comfort and security the immigrants clung to their Old
World cultures and shunned American ways. They often lived in
ghettos, formed their own churches and social clubs, and associated with and married their fellow countrymen. For most groups
it was the second and subsequent generations that gradually gave
up the customs of the immigrants and began the process of assimilation into American society.

Experiences were similar but also different. The slogans "Irish
Need Not Apply," "Christians Only," and "The Chinese Must Go"
signify the hostility of Americans toward the immigrants, but the
degree of hostility differed for each group. Some suffered more than
others. Only the Japanese Americans, for example, were placed in
virtual concentration camps during a period of national crisis.
Moreover, the immigrants brought with them different cultural
heritages, and these largely shaped their responses to the conditions
of the New World. Although each successive generation generally
improved its position in America, the manner and pace of mobility
varied. Some immigrants and their children valued economic success and achieved it quickly, while others defined success differently
and emphasized noneconomic goals. The pace of assimilation also

varied; whereas for some it was rapid, for others it was slow and incomplete. The melting pot has not been fully realized, and, despite enormous expenditures on the part of governmental agencies and existing institutions, ethnic differences remain with us today.

In writing this book we have incurred many debts that we would like to acknowledge. Leo Jacques, Forrest Wilcox, and Tom Everill were helpful research assistants. Panay S. Reyes contributed to, and commented upon, our material on the Filipinos. Michael C. Meyer and Robert D. Schulzinger criticized individual chapters; Myra Dinnerstein, Richard Weiss, and Irwin Unger reviewed the entire manuscript; all made pointed suggestions for improvement. The readers for Dodd, Mead and our editor, Charles Woodford, also made constructive comments, as did Genia Graves. Dorothy Donnelly and Shirley Grover skillfully typed chapter drafts; Wiladene Stickel expertly prepared the final version. Sandra Buchman helped with the proofreading. For the conclusions reached and the errors that still remain we alone are responsible.

LEONARD DINNERSTEIN
DAVID M. REIMERS

ETHNIC AMERICANS
A History of
Immigration and Assimilation

Chapter 1

The Colonial Heritage

NEVER before—and in no other country—have as many varied ethnic groups congregated and amalgamated as they have in the United States. The original seventeenth-century settlers were overwhelmingly English, and it was they who set the tone for American culture. In spite of the English Protestant orientation of society ethnic diversity, even in the colonial period, also characterized the New World. After the 1680s millions of others, including Scotch-Irish, Germans, Scots, Irish, French, Dutch, Italians, Russians, Poles, Scandinavians, Greeks, Chinese, Japanese, Africans, and Latin Americans, eventually emigrated to America. Today most Americans are unable to trace any pure lineage. How many among us can say that he or she is 100 percent French or Dutch or English or German or any of the other strains that built America?

The English were the first Europeans to colonize successfully in the New World. The Dutch, French, and Spanish claimed large empires of land and established settlements earlier, but they were unable to induce significant numbers of their countrymen to leave their homes and live in America. The English, on the other hand zealous in their pursuit of gold and silver, recognized that productive inhabitants increased the wealth of the nation. Even after the restoration of Charles II in 1661, when the English for a time were discouraged from leaving home, England established policies to encourage others to settle in her colonies. Whereas the French and Spanish ruled their overseas domains closely from Paris and Madrid and expected colonists to adhere to the Roman Catholic faith, England, except for the regulation of trade, rarely interfered with the American settlements. The English colonists, almost always short of labor and desirous of populating the wilderness as a buffer zone against the Indians, French, and Spaniards, shared the mother country's enthusiasm for immigrants. As a result of English and colonial attitudes and policies the greatest population movement in history began. Eventually, over 40 million people left Europe in search of the reported golden opportunities of America.

During the colonial period, the vast majority of immigrants were European Protestants who could eventually blend with the dominant English Protestant culture. The 250,000 Scotch-Irish (Presbyterian Scots who settled in Ulster County, Ireland, in the early seventeenth century and whose descendants started emigrating to the American colonies in the early eighteenth century) constituted the largest non-English group, while the 200,000 Germans were the second most significant European minority. About 15,000 Huguenots (Protestants who were evicted from France after the revocation of the Edict of Nantes in 1685 withdrew their privileges of worship there) and considerably smaller numbers of Scots, Dutch, and Swedes rounded out the European population in the colonies. Here and there were small enclaves of Roman Catholics and, in the port cities of Savannah, Charleston, Philadelphia, New York, and Newport scatterings of Jews.

Despite the generally tolerant attitude of the English government toward the newcomers, the English majority in the colonies, which was the dominant group in each area, was not always as gracious as the officials in the mother country. Though they too had come for economic opportunity and freedom to worship God as they thought appropriate, they made no pretense of being tolerant of anyone who deviated significantly from themselves. Hence the arrival of the Scotch-Irish (whom colonists referred to as the "Irish"), the Germans, and others aroused opposition. Americans of every generation have been frightened that newcomers would subvert established customs and undermine the traditions of society, and the dominant group in colonial America was no exception. In 1698 South Carolina passed an act giving bounties to newcomers but exempting the Scotch-Irish and Roman Catholics. At about the same time, Maryland temporarily suspended the importation of Scotch-Irish servants, while Virginia prohibited the sale of more than 20 of them on any one river. In 1729 Pennsylvania placed a 20-shilling duty on each imported servant. "The common fear," one Pennsylvania official said at the time, "is that if they [the Scotch-Irish] thus continue to come they will make themselves proprietors of the Province."

Similar fears have been repeated generation after generation. Only instead of the Scotch-Irish being the "villains," different groups of Americans in different times and places have substituted Italians, Chinese, Jews, blacks, Poles, Puerto Ricans, Irish, Mexicans, and a number of other ethnics. The paradox, which began in colonial America, is this: While on the one hand we have welcomed strangers to work and live among us, on the other hand we have scorned and abused immigrants or minority groups who have deviated from the dominant culture.

Nevertheless, Americans through the late nineteenth century actively recruited European, Asian, and Latin American peoples and emphasized the opportunities available to, rather than the hardships endured by, newcomers. Many colonies sought immigrants, and along with ship companies, they sent agents (newlanders) to Europe to promote their attractions. The newlanders often dressed in fancy attire and wore pocket watches with heavy gold chains to attest to the wealth found in the New World. They carried tales of maids who became ladies, tenants who became landlords, and apprentices who became artisans only a few years after reaching the colonies. But "the best advertisement for the colonies," one historian has written, "was clearly the success of the pioneers. Messages they sent back home inevitably had the effect of removing the last psychological barrier from the minds of many already inclined to leave. Going to America came to mean, in the middle of the [eighteenth] century, not launching into vast unknown, but moving to a country where one's friends and relatives had a home."

The journey to the New World presented travelers with unanticipated hardships. Part of their meager funds had to pay for passage to ports of embarkation, and once there immigrants had to guarantee that the ships would sail to the final destinations on the agreed date. Extra days ashore meant added expenses for food and lodging. Finally on board ship they faced weeks and sometimes months of dismal living conditions on overcrowded and disease-ridden vessels. Shipowners regarded their passengers as freight on which they hoped to maximize profits. The height between decks seldom exceeded five feet, and the immigrants, regardless of sex or marital relation, slept two to three in a berth; one rarely had an area of more than two-by-six feet to call one's own. Despite voyages lasting from six weeks to six months, with many stormy days that forced passengers below deck, portholes for light and ventilation were practically nonexistent. Overcrowding, disease, pestilence, brutal shipmasters, and shortages of food and water added to the tribulations of the ocean crossing. Children under seven frequently became sick and died, and older folk too were often lucky to reach the New World. In 1752 on a ship from the Netherlands to Pennsylvania only 21 out of 340 passengers disembarked; the others had starved to death. On another voyage from Belfast in 1741 6 of the 46 who died "were consumed by the sixty survivors." On yet another ship many drank salt water and their own urine; and on another those who complained of hunger "were put in irons, lashed to the shrouds and flogged."

Despite these hardships, hundreds of thousands did reach their destinations. Many of those who came had lived in poverty in their old homes and were penniless. Shipping agents accepted indigents who signed an indenture agreeing to work in the New World for a period of from three to seven years to pay for their passage money. The immigrants who came in this fashion were often "sold" on board ship, and not infrequently members of the same family wound up with different "masters." Some parents had to "sell their children as if they were cattle," and if parents or spouses died, the remaining members of the family had to serve extra time to pay for the deceased's passage. Unaccompanied children or those whose parents had died during the journey were usually indentured until the age of 21. At the end of their terms the freed servants received a small sum of money, tools, a new suit of clothes, and sometimes land. The sale of indentured servants continued until about 1820. One scholar estimated that anywhere from about one-half to two-thirds of the white immigrants came to the English colonies in this manner.

Most of the colonists before the 1660s came directly from England. They laid the foundation and set the direction for the future development of American society. The settlement at Jamestown in 1607 resulted from the visions of some London-based fortune hunters who dreamed of large profits. By 1622 famines, pestilence, and Indian troubles practically destroyed the colony, and the English crown assumed possession.

In New England both Pilgrims and Puritans considered themselves good Christians. Like so many others who would follow, economic factors also influenced their decision to settle there. They were plagued by a faltering European economy, and the move to the New World provided the opportunity to implant their own way of life in a virgin territory and to improve their economic fortunes.

No group, no matter how large its numbers, was ever as significant in the development of the United States as were the Pilgrims
and Puritans. Their ideology emphasized the importance of the Protestant faith, diligent application to work, and individual accomplishment. They often paid homage to those who attained great
wealth. They cherished the Anglo-Saxon legal heritage and revered
the written compact. They brought the English language to the New
World. All of these aspects of their culture were firmly implanted
on American soil, and they laid the foundations for American
society. Every succeeding immigrant group that came to the English
colonies, and later to the United States, had to absorb these aspects
of the dominant culture before they in turn would be accepted as
"Americans."

After Charles I succeeded his father, James I, on the English
throne in 1625, domestic concerns prevented him from giving much
attention to the colonies. He did, nevertheless, grant an area of land
north of Virginia to George Calvert, Lord Baltimore, which was
christened Maryland. Calvert, a Roman Catholic, hoped the colony
would be financially profitable and serve as a haven for his coreligionists. Unfortunately, he died before actually receiving the grant
from the king, and the deed went to his son Cecilius, who embarked
upon a voyage to the New World in 1634. From the beginning
there were large numbers of Protestants in Maryland, and to protect Catholics in case of eventual discrimination Lord Baltimore
urged passage of the Toleration Act in 1649; it granted freedom of
religion to all who believed in the divinity of Jesus Christ. Five years
later, however, under the domination of a Protestant legislature the
act was repealed and Catholics were denied the protection of the
law. The repeal signified quite strikingly how the colonists, and in
later centuries other Protestants, regarded the Roman Catholic faith.

Maryland was the last New World colony established by England
before the domestic turbulence of the 1640s routed and then led to
the beheading of King Charles I. Oliver Cromwell's protectorate
lasted only until 1661, when Charles II, son of the dethroned
monarch, restored the crown to England.

After 1661 the new reign discouraged emigration. The mercantile theory, which held sway for the next century, dictated that
the wealth of nations lay in their inhabitants and their production
and that loss of population meant, in effect, loss of riches. The

English colonists, therefore, had to seek other sources of population. In 1662 the Royal African Slave Company received a monopoly from the crown and began importing African slaves in increasing numbers. By 1680, however, William Penn received a grant of land from King Charles II and went to Europe to recruit settlers directly.

Penn printed hundreds of pamphlets in English, German, French, and Dutch describing the wonders of Pennsylvania. Pennsylvania, the Europeans were told over and over again, was a land where crops never failed, where game roamed aplenty, where abundant supplies of wood stood ready for use in building houses, barns, and furniture, where religious freedom was guaranteed to all, and where no political restrictions harassed dissenters. Moreover, the colony promised universal male suffrage, a humane penal code, and no compulsory military service. As one historian later wrote, "Pennsylvania was in truth a land of milk and honey." No wonder that more immigrants sailed for Philadelphia than for all other ports combined in the colonial era.

Penn's promotional efforts appealed particularly to those affected by the intermittent wars in the German states during the seventeenth century. German Pietists and subsequently members of the Lutheran and Reformed churches left Europe for the beckoning opportunities in the New World. As a result of vigorous advertising, Pennsylvania became the mecca for German immigrants, though Germans settled in all of the other colonies as well.

Members of various German sects were found in English America, but the majority were members of the Lutheran or Reformed churches. They came to the New World for a combination of economic, religious, and political reasons: Some came to escape persecution in states where tyrannical princes had different faiths; others came because crop failures, famines, or continuous wars made prospects for the future seem bleak. The relaxation of emigration restrictions in Switzerland and the German states in the eighteenth century also stimulated emigration as did glowing letters from friends and relatives who had already gone to the English colonies.

Wherever the Germans went, they prospered. Their concern for their property was proverbial, and it was often said that a German took better care of his cows than his children. After settling on good lands the Germans built sturdy houses and barns and tilled their farms with diligence and enthusiasm. One historian has written that they "produced in their children not only the *habits* of labor but a *love* of it." They fed their stock well, exercised frugality in diet and dress, and were known for their thrift, industry, punctuality, and sense of justice.

But the colonial Germans had little desire to blend with the rest of the population. They kept to themselves, continued speaking German, attended their own churches, and rarely took the opportunity to become citizens of the British Empire. They maintained their own culture and feared that the use of English and contact with other groups would completely Anglicize their children. Because of their aloofness they antagonized the dominant English group in the colonies, especially in Pennsylvania, who viewed them as dangerous elements in the community. Even Benjamin Franklin, an urbane and decent man, disliked the Germans who poured into Pennsylvania in the eighteenth century, and demanded: "Why should the *Palatine Boors* be suffered to swarm into our Settlements, and by herding together, establish their Language and Manners, to the Exclusion of ours? Why should *Pennsylvania,* founded by the *English,* become a Colony of *Aliens,* who will shortly be so numerous as to Germanize us instead of our Anglifying them . . .?"

The Scotch-Irish, like the Germans, were Protestants who left their homes for religious and economic reasons. In the late seventeenth century English mercantile laws had prohibited the exportation of Irish woolens except to England and Wales, and this nearly crippled Ulster's profitable foreign trade. Then successive increases in rents, termination of farm leases, poor harvests, curtailed supplies of flax to linen manufacturers, increased food costs, and restrictions precluding Presbyterians from holding political offices piled woe upon woe. Furthermore, the English Parliament decreed that the children of all Protestants not married in the Church of England must be declared bastards. The absurdity of this ruling also resulted in " 'many persons of undoubted reputation' [being] prosecuted in the bishops courts as fornicators for cohabitating with their own wives." But not until 1717, when the fourth successive year of droughts ruined crops, were serious preparations begun for the migration to the New World.

The first group of Scotch-Irish to leave their homeland may have been motivated by religious as well as economic conditions, but, thereafter, glowing shipping advertisements, letters from friends and relatives in the colonies, and poor economic conditions in Ireland

sparked further emigration. Intensive and protracted periods of
Scotch-Irish emigration to the American colonies correlated with
the ebb and flow of prosperity in the linen industry in Ireland.

The original Scotch-Irish settlers went to Worcester, Massachusetts, and Londonderry, New Hampshire, where they met a chilly
reception. Pennsylvania, on the other hand, because of its tolerance
readily received them. Perhaps even more importantly, the boats
carrying flaxseed went to Philadelphia, and so the Scotch-Irish went
there too.

Most of the Scotch-Irish arrived as indentured servants, but once
their periods of service ended, they moved to the frontier, and their
settlements dotted the outskirts of Pennsylvania, Maryland, Virginia, and the Carolinas. Unlike the Germans, the Scotch-Irish were
forever on the move.

The Scotch-Irish, although a colonial minority, left a mark on
American society that remains to this day. Wherever they went, the
church and the schoolhouse followed. Devoutly religious and with
an intense desire for learning, they stressed the importance of an
educated ministry and the dissemination of knowledge. Their stern
morality pervaded the American scene. The Presbyterians frowned
on dancing, card playing, the theater, breaking the Sabbath by any
diversion, and engaging in frivolous pastimes. Later contact with
other immigrant groups eventually mitigated the harshness of
Scotch-Irish codes, but they still persist to some extent among some
of the more devout Methodists and Southern Baptists, many of
whom are descended from the colonial Scotch-Irish. Scotch-Irish
frequently became Methodists and Baptists on the frontier because
of their inability to find trained Presbyterian ministers and because
the New World loosened many Old World ties while facilitating
new associations.

Fewer numbers of other ethnic groups also populated the English
colonies. Because they constituted a small percentage of the total
population their influence, as well as their continued existence as
separate groups, was not lasting. About 15,000 Huguenots settled
in virtually every region of the colonies but concentrated in the port
cities, especially Charleston, South Carolina. As a group they
included a high proportion of professionals, merchants, and craftsmen and a very small number of indentured servants. Although
Protestants, they met with considerable hostility from the dominant
groups in their communities. Two or three generations of continuous

intermarriage dissolved most distinguishable French traits, however. Sizable numbers of Scots from Scotland (as contrasted with the Scotch-Irish from Ireland) came to the British colonies after 1763, primarily for economic reasons. The Dutch in New York, the Swedes in Delaware, the few hundred Jews, and perhaps 25,000 Roman Catholics also maintained cultures different from those of the dominant groups, but they exercised a rather negligible influence on society compared to the major identifiable peoples.

In sum, the American colonies, settled predominantly by the English, had two major European minorities—the Germans and the Scotch-Irish, both Protestant—and a mélange of other peoples, mostly Protestant. The two major non-European minorities—the Indians and the blacks—were relegated to an inferior status. The white minorities eventually blended with the dominant English culture, and although there were varieties of Protestant sects, the children and grandchildren learned to tolerate differences within Protestantism.

The pattern of minority life developed in the English colonies in the seventeenth century set the standard for future European minorities in this country. The English colonists and later Americans of the majority group appreciated the labor that the newcomers could provide, but they expected the immigrants to absorb the dominant customs while shedding their own as quickly as possible. Minority group members were sought for their labor yet were despised for their ignorance of English, their attachment to cultures and faiths prevalent in the Old World, and their lack of knowledge of the American way.

The War for Independence from England and the formation of a new American government had a nationalizing effect on the formerly separate colonies. Many of the immigrants—and their children—were now quite proud to regard themselves as Americans rather than transplanted Europeans. Some ethnic groups—notably the Germans who lived between the Delaware and Susquehanna rivers in Pennsylvania—resisted Americanization for a longer time than the others, but sooner or later most of them assimilated. The Napoleonic Wars, which began in the 1790s and lasted through 1815, slowed the pace of emigration from Europe, and this hiatus quickened the Americanizing process among the immigrant stock in the United States.

Chapter 2

The Old Immigrants

T HE century and a half following the Napoleonic Wars in Europe witnessed the greatest migration of peoples in the history of the world. Originally sparked by the Industrial Revolution, which forced peasants off the land and into the cities, the movement also gained momentum from many other factors in the social history of Europe. The European population doubled between 1750 and 1850. At the same time, intensified religious persecutions and a relaxation of emigration restrictions in various European nations combined with a transportation revolution to facilitate the movement of those who wanted to travel. Meanwhile, receptive countries in South Africa, Oceania, and North and South America sought people to exploit resources. Finally, two devastating world wars uprooted millions. More than 60 million people left their native countries during this period. Some went only from one European or Asian country to another, but others sought riches in Africa, Asia, and South America. More than 15 million went to Canada, Argentina, and Brazil. About two-thirds of the migrants, who were primarily European but included considerable numbers of Asians and Latin Americans, chose the United States as their destination. Their arrival would be one of the most significant factors shaping the destiny of this country.

In the years between 1820 and 1930 America received more than 37 million immigrants, mostly from Europe. An analysis of time periods reveals that those coming from northern and western Europe predominated through the 1880s, while the southern and eastern Europeans overshadowed the others after the 1880s. As Table 2–1 shows, the great surge came after 1880.

Table 2-1. Immigration to America, 1820–1930

Decade	Germany	Ireland	England, Scotland, Wales	Scandinavia	Italy	Austro-Hungary	Russia & Baltic States	Totals
1820	968	3,614	2,410	23	30		14	8,385
1821–30	6,761	50,724	25,079	260	409		75	143,439
1831–40	152,454	207,654	75,810	2,264	2,253		277	599,125
1841–50	434,626	780,719	267,044	13,122	1,970		551	1,713,251
1851–60	951,657	914,119	423,929	24,680	9,231		457	2,598,214
1861–70	827,468	435,697	607,076	126,392	11,725	7,800	2,515	2,314,824
1871–80	718,182	436,871	548,043	242,934	55,795	72,969	39,287	2,812,191
1881–90	1,452,970	655,540	807,357	655,494	307,309	362,719	213,282	5,246,613
1891–1900	505,152	388,416	271,538	371,512	651,873	574,069	505,281	3,687,564
1901–10	341,498	339,065	525,950	505,324	2,045,877	2,145,266	1,597,308	8,795,386
1911–20	143,945	146,199	341,408	203,452	1,209,524	901,656	921,957	5,735,811
1921–30	412,202	220,564	330,168	198,210	455,315	214,806	89,423	4,107,209
Totals	5,947,883	4,579,182	4,225,812	2,343,667	4,751,311	4,279,285	3,370,427	

All of these people, of course, cannot be treated in one chapter. Hence a discussion of the different groups has been divided into three roughly chronological periods. The so-called old immigrants, those of northern and western Europe, will be considered in this chapter along with the French Canadians and the Chinese, whose main entry occurred in the nineteenth century. The next chapter deals both with the "new" immigrants from southern and eastern Europe and with the Japanese, whose major emigration occurred roughly between 1880 and 1920. Later chapters deal with (1) the Spanish-speaking migrants from Mexico and the Caribbean, whose presence is, for the most part, a twentieth-century phenomenon; (2) the refugees coming as a result of Hitler's persecutions, World War II, and the cold war; and (3) the new immigrants who have become eligible for admission to the United States because of congressional action since 1965.

Although foreigners arrived in the United States throughout the nineteenth century, statistics reveal that before 1880 the bulk was concentrated in two major periods: from 1845 to 1854, when more than 3 million persons landed at American ports, and from 1865 to 1875, when the numbers reached almost 3.5 million. Aside from these years mass immigration is a phenomenon of the half century between 1880 and 1930. In the first period the Irish and Germans exceeded all others; in the second period the English and Scandinavians figured heavily along with the first two; and after 1880 all of these groups were joined, and then swamped, by southern and eastern European emigrants, who propelled American immigration totals to new heights.

Most immigrants came essentially because of poor economic conditions in Europe and prospects for a better life in the United States. Local concerns and variations, the pace of industrialization on the Continent, the disruptions of World War I, and the restrictive immigration quotas of the 1920s had much to do with the timing of the emigrants' departure. In Great Britain the industrial change began in the eighteenth century, and the British clearly dominated American immigration statistics until the 1840s; in the German states the transformation of the social order made its most profound impact in the second third of the nineteenth century; hence the Germans began to move only after 1830; and in Scandinavia the decade of the 1880s, with its economic upheavals,

proved most significant for migration. Nevertheless, the peaks and
troughs in foreign arrivals after 1819 correspond roughly with the
fluctuations in the business cycles in the United States. Good years
such as 1854, 1873, 1892, 1907, and 1921 were high points for
immigration, but they were followed by industrial depressions that
resulted in correspondingly low totals for new entrants.

People do not cross continents and oceans without considerable
thought, nor do they uproot themselves from family, friends, and
familiar terrain without significant strain. The motivation to emigrate must be overwhelming before the fateful step is taken. In the
nineteenth century, as in the seventeenth and eighteenth, poverty
was the chief spur to movement. One eminent historian has written:
"The most powerful factor impelling emigration was an extraordinary increase in population, preceding the ability of agriculture
to feed it or of industry to give it jobs." The industrial and agricultural revolutions wrought such profound changes in Europe that
large numbers of people were forced by circumstances beyond their
control to relinquish ancestral dwellings and move to where they
could find jobs. Yet one cannot ignore the variety of other propelling
reasons. Religious intolerance, demeaning social gradations, political
upheavals—all these pushed people across the Atlantic, and the
ubiquitous "American letters" describing the Garden of Eden in the
New World pulled countless thousands to America. Nevertheless, it
must still be acknowledged that the economic factor was the most
compelling for the majority of emigrants.

The Irish were the first of the impoverished Europeans to leave
in the nineteenth century. The Irish Poor Law of 1838, the enclo-
sure movement on the land, and finally the great famine at the end
of the 1840s, which ravaged the potato crops and brought untold
misery and starvation to millions, combined to increase emigration.
A French observer who had visited both America and Ireland before
the Great Hunger said the condition of the Irish was worse than
that of black slaves. He concluded: "There is no doubt that the
most miserable of English paupers is better fed and clothed than
the most prosperous of Irish laborers." As hundreds of thousands
starved to death during the famine, one of the few lucrative trades
left in Tipperary was the sale of coffin mountings and hinges. One
man lamented of the suffering, "Every day furnished victims, and
the living hear, and endeavor to drive from their minds, as soon as

they can, the horrifying particulars that are related. I have this day, returning to my house, witnessed more than one person lying in our district at this moment unburied. I have known of bodies here remaining in the mountainous parts, neglected for more than eight days." Many of the destitute Irish went to England, some to South America, but more than a million came to the United States. The majority of these people remained in the port cities of New York and Boston, where they landed because they were too poor to move any farther; but others traveled west. As conditions improved in Ireland in the middle of the 1850s, emigration subsided, but another potato rot in 1863 and still another famine in the 1880s swelled the Irish emigration statistics. Almost 4 million Irish came to the United States in the nineteenth century. Their impact in this country has far exceeded both their numbers and their percentage of the population.

Along with the Irish came the Germans. But, unlike the Irish, they continued to be the largest ethnic group arriving in all but three of the years between 1854 and 1894. Before the end of the century more than 5 million Germans reached the United States; in the twentieth century another 2 million came. The exodus, at first primarily from the rural and agricultural southern and western regions of Germany, fits the general pattern of immigration. Crop failures, high rents and prices, and the changeover to an industrial economy stimulated the move. Conditions were not as bad as in impoverished Ireland, but they were bad enough. One observer told of the "poor wretches" on the road to Strasbourg: "There they go slowly along; their miserable tumbrils—drawn by such starved dropping beasts, that your only wonder is, how can they possibly reach Havre alive." Relatives and friends who went first to America wrote, for the most part, glowing letters, and this in turn stimulated further waves. Rich farmers who saw a bleak future in Germany, poor ones who had no future, peasants, paupers whom the state paid to leave, a handful of disappointed revolutionaries after 1848, and an assortment of artisans and professionals came in the 1840s and 1850s.

In late 1854 reports circulated in the German states of large numbers of shipwrecks and cholera epidemics at sea that resulted in death rates as high as 50 percent. At about the same time, nativist agitation in the United States reached a peak; and the American economy turned downward. These factors curtailed immigration in the late 1850s, and then came the Civil War, which deterred people already beset with troubles enough of their own.

Between 1866 and 1873, however, a combination of American prosperity and European depression once again increased German emigration totals. Congressional passage of the Homestead Act granting free land to settlers, the convulsions in the German states due to Bismarck's wars in the 1860s, the high conscription rate, and low wages at home also prompted German emigration. When the United States suffered a severe depression between 1873 and 1879, immigration figures were correspondingly depressed. But when the American economy improved, it immediately affected anxious Europeans, who descended heavily upon our shores in the early 1880s. Germans who believed that prosperity would never be theirs at home left in record numbers, which peaked in 1882 when more than 250,000 passed through the immigration stations here. The American depressions of the late 1880s and 1893–1894 cut emigration sharply, but by then an improved industrial economy in Germany provided greater opportunities than in the past, and fewer Germans felt compelled to seek their fortunes in the New World.

The Scandinavians, the largest northwestern European group, after the British and the Germans, to populate America in the nineteenth century, increased their numbers in the United States markedly after the Civil War. The first group of nineteenth-century Scandinavians arrived in the autumn of 1825, when about 50 Norwegians settled in Kendall, New York, about 30 miles southwest of Rochester. In 1841 a Swedish colony developed in Pine Lake, Wisconsin. During the next decades, Scandinavians continued to come but never in the numbers that either the Irish or Germans did. For example, Scandinavian immigration totaled only 2,830 in 1846 and not much more in 1865. After 1868, however, annual immigration from Norway, Sweden, Denmark, and Finland passed the 10,000 mark. Jacob Riis, the famous social reformer and friend of Theodore Roosevelt, for example, left Denmark for America in 1870. Like so many other immigrants, he arrived with little but "a pair of strong hands, and stubbornness enough to do for two; [and] also a strong belief that in a free country, free from the dominion of custom, of caste, as well as of men, things would somehow come right in the end." Other Danes and Scandinavians obviously agreed, for annual immigration from Scandinavia did not fall below the 10,000 mark until the disruptions caused by World War I. In the 1920s, when other Europeans resumed their exodus, the Scandinavians joined them.

As in the case of the Irish and the Germans, Scandinavian immigration can be correlated to a large extent with economic conditions at home and in the United States. Sweden enjoyed a period of good crop production between 1850 and 1864; the years between 1865 and 1868, however, culminated in a great famine that coincided with particularly bountiful times in the United States. During those three years, emigrants increased sharply, doubling from 1865 to 1866 and tripling from 9,000 in 1867 to 27,000 in 1868. The exodus from Norway can be explained almost wholly by the industrial transformation and the consequent disruptions at home. Norwegian migration can be grouped into three significant periods: from 1866 to 1873, when 111,000 people came; from 1879 to 1893, when the figures went over 250,000; and from 1900 to 1910, when the numbers totaled about 200,000. Industrialism came earlier in Denmark than in either Norway or Sweden, and the rural upheaval sent people into the cities and towns. But there were simply not enough jobs for those willing to work, and many artisans and skilled laborers sought opportunities in America. By 1920 U.S. census figures recorded 190,000 Danish-born in this country.

Although economic factors overshadow all others for the Scandinavians, it would be misleading, except in the case of the Danes, who had no serious political or religious problems, to overlook social difficulties as motivating forces for the emigrants. In Sweden and Norway church and state were aligned, and both dissenters and nonconformists were penalized. There was no universal suffrage, and tightened conscription laws bothered many young men; one scholar noted a particularly high proportion of emigrants among those eligible for military service in Sweden in the 1880s. Swedes in particular also abhorred the hierarchy of titles and the rigidly defined class system. After living in the United States, one Swede wrote home that his "cap [is not] worn out from lifting it in the presence of gentlemen. There is no class distinction between high and low, rich and poor, no make-believe, no 'title-sickness,' or artificial ceremonies. . . . Everybody lives in peace and prosperity."

Another compelling, perhaps decisive, reason was something called "American fever." After Europeans left their homelands, they wrote to their compatriots and described the wonders of America, or the "land of Canaan." Nowhere did these letters have a greater impact than in the Scandinavian countries. They were passed carefully from family to family, published intact in the local newspapers, and discussed avidly from the pulpits on Sundays. The continuous influx of favorable mail inspired whole villages with the fervent desire to emigrate to America. Not all of the letters from the United States glowed with praise, however, and many in fact did complain of the adjustment to the New World. But as one emigrant succinctly put it, "Norway cannot be compared to America any more than a desert can be compared to a garden in full bloom."

The Irish, the Germans, and the Scandinavians comprised the main non-English European immigrants during this period, but others chose to emigrate to the New World for similar reasons. Religious dissenters from the Netherlands founded colonies in Michigan and Iowa in the 1840s, but by coincidence the timing of their departure corresponds with potato blight and economic depression at home. By 1902 more than 135,000 Dutch most of whom had arrived in the 1880s and 1890s, lived in the United States.

Two other groups, the French Canadians and the Chinese, also made significant impressions on the United States. Overpopulation at home and the diminishing size of agricultural plots that had been divided and subdivided for generations finally induced French Canadians to start emigrating in the 1830s, although most left Canada between 1860 and 1900. The emigrants totaled approximately 300,000 and settled for the most part in the mill villages and factory towns of New England.

The discovery of gold in California in 1849 had a great impact on the Chinese. News of the strike reached China via American merchant ships, but only the people of Toishan, a depressed agricultural province about 150 miles northwest of Hong Kong, responded. Toishan's agricultural output could feed its population for only about one-third of the year, and floods and typhoons frequently devasted the community. As a result, many Toishanese moved into commercial activities and came in contact with Westerners in Hong Kong and Canton, the two major cities closest to this agricultural province. They were receptive, therefore, to the opportunity for enrichment in the United States, and a number of the more adventurous males made the long journey. Only a few women accompanied the men. During subsequent years, more than half of all the Chinese in the United States came from Toishan, and a large percentage of the others came from areas surrounding that province. Lack of contact with Americans probably deterred other Chinese from going to the United States.

The tremendous physical and economic growth of the United States in the nineteenth century made it mandatory for Americans to turn to the new settlers and laborers for cheap labor to plow fields, build canals and railroads, dig mines, and man machinery in fledgling factories. Without the newcomers the vast riches of the nation could not have been exploited quickly.

Fantastic efforts and inducements were made to lure Europeans, French Canadians, Chinese, and, later, Latin Americans, to the United States. Their strong backs and steadfast enterprise were necessary to turn American dreams into American accomplishments. At the forefront of these efforts were the state and territorial governments, the railroads, and the various emigrant-aid societies, which were buttressed by federal legislation.

Just as the Atlantic seaboard states had made efforts in the colonial period to attract settlers, so in the nineteenth century practically every state and territory of the American West, plus several others, sought to entice select groups of Europeans to their area. More people meant more schools and post offices, larger federal appropriations for internal improvements, larger markets for goods, faster economic development, "and the speedy arrival of the eagerly-desired railroad."

In 1845 Michigan became the first state legislature to provide for the appointment of an immigration agent to recruit settlers at the New York docks, and Wisconsin followed suit seven years later. After the Civil War, though, the competition among states for Europeans intensified, and efforts to attract them expanded on a vast scale. At least 33 states and territorial governments eventually set up immigration bureaus, advertised in European and American foreign-language newspapers, sent agents to northern and western Europe, and published their brochures, guidebooks, and maps in English, Welsh, German, Dutch, French, Norwegian, and Swedish. Each state elaborated upon its virtues, "the likes of which," one historian has written, "had never been known—except to other states seeking immigration." Minnesota, proud of its "beautiful lakes, forests, prairies and salubrious climate"—and quiet about its subzero winters—offered two prizes for the best essays on the state as a place for European immigrants and then published them in seven languages. Kansas specifically exempted the Mennonites from militia service, and thousands of them moved there from Central Europe in the 1870s. In 1870 the movement came to a head when several Midwestern governors organized a national immigration convention at Indianapolis. Delegates from 22 states and the District of Columbia attended the meeting. They discussed how the federal government could be more helpful in recruitment, and they petitioned Congress to establish a national immigration bureau. The heyday for the state bureaus ended with the depression of 1873, but several continued into the 1880s and 1890s. On the eve of World War I Louisiana officials still distributed enticing brochures in several foreign languages to those disembarking at New Orleans, and the legislatures of Michigan, Wisconsin, and South Dakota continued to make appropriations to induce foreigners to settle in their states.

The railroads worked as hard as the states to attract immigrants, and, in fact, in the words of historian Carl Wittke, were "probably the most important promotional agencies at work for some years around the turn of the century." After 1854, but especially in the 1870s and 1880s, most of the transcontinental railroads actively promoted immigration to the areas where they owned lands. The more people who settled in any given location, the more business and profits for the trains. Crops and merchandise would have to be moved and, with additional markets and sources of labor, industrialists and governmental aid would surely follow. Like the states, the railroads subsidized agents in Europe, advertised and printed brochures in many languages, and played up the virtues of their respective territories. In addition, some gave free or reduced passage to prospective settlers, established immigrant receiving houses near their terminals, and built churches and schools for fledgling communities.

The first railroad to seek foreigners aggressively, the Illinois Central, inaugurated its program in 1854. The line sent special agents to the German states and the Scandinavian countries, and these men attended fairs and church services, arranged meetings, advertised in the local press, and promised fabulous inducements to prospective settlers. Not only did they help secure ocean passage, but they also provided free railroad transportation to Illinois to prospective land purchasers and their families. If the immigrant then bought land from the company, the Illinois Central allowed for long-term payments at 6 percent interest, gave discounts to the farmer for shipping his future crops on the line, and agreed to pay all land taxes until payments were completed. Immigrants preferred buying railroad lands to homesteading free governmental acreage because of these inducements as well as the fact that the railroads often offered choicer properties.

While the Illinois Central had almost completed its efforts in 1870, most railroads were inaugurating their land and development bureaus. Some functioned as agents for states; the Burlington line, for example, represented Iowa, and the Northern Pacific line acted as Oregon's East Coast representative. They also published monthly newsletters in various northern and western European languages, and the Northern Pacific even set up its own newspapers in Germany, Switzerland, and England. From 1882 to 1883 alone the company printed 635,590 copies of its publications in English, Swedish, Norwegian, Danish, Dutch, and German and also distributed a monthly newsletter for immigrants, *Northwest*. The Burlington's efforts resulted in the sale of nearly 3 million acres in Iowa and Nebraska, and the Northern Pacific is credited with having more than doubled the population of Minnesota, the Dakotas, Montana, and the Pacific Northwest between 1880 and 1900.

Working together with the railroads and state agencies to encourage immigration were the various emigrant-aid societies. But unlike the state agencies and railroads these semiphilanthropic organizations were more interested in assisting departing Europeans and easing their travails in a foreign land by providing interpreters, clean boardinghouses, and employment bureaus in the United States than in encouraging them to come to America. This aid was clearly necessary, for as one Swedish emigration agent explained, "most of the emigrants are entirely ignorant about how to come to America. . . ."

Numerous steamship lines also vigorously promoted their own interests by seeking out immigrants. By 1882 48 steamship companies traversed the Atlantic, each competing furiously with the other for the immigrant traffic. Fares were relatively cheap. One could go from England to the United States, for instance, for about $12 to $15 and from Copenhagen to New York for about $30. Publicity and services attracted customers. The Red Star, Anchor, and Hamburg-American lines, among others, received patronage by establishing more than 6,500 agencies in the United States to sell prepaid tickets. As early as the 1850s the Irish were sending more than a million dollars a year—about half in prepaid tickets—to their relatives and friends at home, and other immigrant groups were no less diligent. In the 1880s estimates are that most of the Scandinavians emigrating to the United States came on prepaid tickets or purchased them with money specifically sent for that purpose. Although there are no exact statistics available, historians assume that from 25 to 70 percent of all immigrants in the late nineteenth and early twentieth centuries received either prepaid tickets from the United States or money specifically designated to facilitate the journey.

Although the companies vied for the immigrant traffic, few felt compelled to make the voyage comfortable for steerage passengers. Before the 1850s immigrants came in sailing vessels quite similar to those the colonists had arrived in a century or two earlier and under similar filthy conditions. The average journey across the Atlantic took about 44 days, although voyages of four to six months were not uncommon. Like their forebears, many of those arriving in the nineteenth century, especially on English packets, which had been built for carrying cargo and not people, suffered almost inhuman treatment. Overcrowding, filth, stench, and poor ventilation were standard on almost all vessels, and tales of starvation and brutal assaults stand out in the accounts of many of the crossings. Over and over again one reads of the lack of sufficient food and water, of crew members beating and kicking helpless passengers, and of rampant disease. Dysentery, cholera, typhoid fever, lice, and "the itch" abounded. Those in steerage slept and ate on wooden bunks, which looked like dog kennels, and had straw-stuffed mattresses. One mid-century ship from Ireland possessed only 36 berths for 260 people; another had only 32 for 276. After one Irish ship had docked in New Orleans, customs officials found passengers and pigs lying together in "filth and feculent matter." Wanton beatings, assaults, and animal-like treatment by crew members were recorded frequently. One observer wrote that "it was a daily occurrence to see starving women and children fight for the food which was brought to the dogs and the pigs that were kept on the deck of the ship." An emigrants' guide in 1851 likened the fate of steerage travelers to those on the African slavers; and as a surgeon who had served on six emigrant ships wrote, "the torments of hell might in some degree resemble the suffering of emigrants, but crime was punished in hell, whereas in an emigrant ship it flourished without check or retribution."

With the advent of steamships, however, conditions and amenities improved. The average crossing lasted 14 days in 1867 and only 5½ days in 1897. On the steamers everyone had his own berth, women slept separately from men, and the galley provided three meals a day. Overcrowding and foul odors still existed, and the turbulence of the North Atlantic still forced many a passenger to his knees to pray for divine assistance; but temporary inconvenience for ten days could be endured with greater ease than that of the much longer and more difficult passage on the sailing ships. Moreover, between 1855 and 1875 both European and American governments established more stringent rules to improve conditions for emigrants and restrict abuses by shipmasters.

Immigrant traffic followed commercial routes. Because of the Canadian timber trade a number of vessels, mostly British ships carrying Irish, went to Boston. British officials also concluded that the fastest way to send mail to Canada was via Boston, which also explains in large part how the Irish wound up in Massachusetts. The Mississippi trade made New Orleans the major Southern port and also resulted in its receiving more immigrants than any other Southern city. But the journey to Louisiana took an extra two or three weeks; moreover, the climate in the lower South was muggy, and the possibility of disease was great, so that most Europeans shunned that route. New York, the nation's major commercial center, also served as its chief immigration depot. From 1816 on it accommodated more than 70 percent of the newcomers, and its reception centers at Castle Garden and later at Ellis Island became world famous.

Regulation of foreigners entering British America had been a function of the individual colonies and later, by tradition, of the states. The federal government did require the collecting of vital statistics in 1819 but otherwise allowed immigrants to enter unfettered until 1882, when it imposed additional regulations.

New York State, where most of the newcomers landed, passed a series of laws, beginning in 1824, requiring ship captains to post bonds indemnifying the state for any expenses incurred in connection with paupers disembarking there. Later the state required a $1 head tax on steerage passengers to finance an immigrant hospital. In 1847 New York established the State Board of Commissioners of

Immigration. The law creating the board granted the commissioners the power to collect vital statistics, board and inspect incoming ships, establish and manage an immigrant hospital, and quarantine those who had communicable diseases. The commissioners, who served without pay, made every effort to assist the newly arrived foreigners. In 1855 they set up Castle Garden, a model reception center, through which everyone disembarking in New York had to pass. In this way the foreigners were counted, and their ages, occupations, religions, and the value of property they brought with them were recorded. The immigrants at the centers had to bathe with soap and water, and afterward they could purchase items like bread, milk, and coffee and use the extensive kitchen facilities to prepare their own food. Officials encouraged everyone to leave the depot within hours of arrival, but those who wished could sleep overnight in the galleries. Beds were not provided, but a few thousand could be lodged. Immigration officials had already inspected and licensed numerous New York City boardinghouses, and they posted lists of suitable accommodations. Before this time many "greenhorns," as the immigrants were called, had been fleeced by boardinghouse agents and cheated by phony ticket sellers and other swindlers. To counteract this Castle Garden also provided money exchanges and railroad and canal ticket booths for those going inland and disseminated information about the United States and employment opportunities throughout the country.

Castle Garden remained the nation's chief immigrant depot for more than 35 years. In 1876 the United States Supreme Court forbade New York State to collect bonds from ship captains on the ground that they were equivalent to head taxes, and for the next six years New York State financed the reception center out of its general funds. In 1882 Congress levied a 50-cent head tax on newcomers and defrayed New York's expenses out of the monies collected. In 1890, though, the federal government finally took charge of immigration and relieved the states of their role in this area. Ellis Island replaced the abandoned Castle Garden as the gateway to America for millions of Europeans.

Once through Castle Garden, and later Ellis Island, foreigners dispersed quickly. Those too poor to go anywhere else remained in New York. Others, determined to reach the wooded regions and fertile prairies of the Midwest, obtained the necessary railroad or canal tickets and proceeded on their journeys. A favorite route began

with a boat ride up the Hudson River to Albany and then across the
Erie Canal to Buffalo, then by water, rail, or wagon to the ultimate
destination. Most of the nineteenth-century newcomers from Germany and Scandinavia wanted their own farms; the Homestead
Act, the invitations from the states and the railroads, and the letters
from relatives drew them to the north central plains, where land was
either free or cheap. (As late as 1879 some Wisconsin land sold for
50 cents an acre.)

Those who were too poor, like many Irish, to finance any trip
once they had arrived in America, accepted the offers of canal and
railroad builders to be taken along to construction projects. Eventually, as a result, pockets of Irish existed in every region of the
country. Most Irish, however, remained in the port cities where they
landed or in their environs. By the end of the nineteenth century
Irish colonies existed in San Francisco and New Orleans, but the
majority were in Massachusetts, New York, Pennsylvania, and
Illinois.

The Germans, who, as was noted previously, were the most
numerous of the nineteenth-century immigrants, had originally
hoped to plant a new Germany in America: Missouri in the 1830s,
Texas in the 1840s, and Wisconsin in the 1850s were the states
that they had hoped to make their own. American expansion and
ideology, however, quickly frustrated such visions. Native Americans were unwilling to allow any group to carve out its own exclusive territory in the United States, and subsequent waves of immigrants showed no respect or tolerance for the wishes of those
Germans who wanted to insulate their settlements. Germans toiled
as farmers in rural areas and as both skilled and unskilled laborers
in the urban communities. Nearly half of them settled in Illinois,
Michigan, Missouri, Iowa, and Wisconsin, but Texas published
its laws in the German language in 1843, and Germans comprised
one-fifth of the white population there four years later. Many of
the counties of west Texas owe their beginnings to German immigrants, and by 1900 estimates attribute about one-third of the state's
white population to German origins. Germans also dominated the
foreign-born statistics and lent a particular flavor to St. Louis, Cincinnati, and Milwaukee. Even in New York City they outnumbered
all other foreign elements in the nineteenth century. One observer
described New York's *Kleindeutschland* in the 1850s, "Life in
Kleindeutschland is almost the same as in the Old Country. . . .

There is not a single business which is not run by Germans. Not only the shoemakers, tailors, barbers, physicians, grocers, and innkeepers are German, but the pastors and priests as well. . . . The resident of *Kleindeutschland* need not even know English in order to make a living." In fact, by 1900 Germans still constituted the single largest ethnic minority in 27 states.

Before 1890 the Scandinavians went mostly to the wheatgrowing regions of Illinois, Wisconsin, Iowa, Minnesota, the Dakotas, Kansas, and Nebraska. The rich and fertile soil, the open spaces, and the harsh winter climate reminded them of their European homes, and with each successive wave of settlement there was the added attraction of living near friends and relatives from the old country. The solicitations from the actively recruiting states and railroads steered them into the Midwest, and the boom times of the early 1880s kept them there. Minnesota's population, buttressed by a heavy migration from Germany and Scandinavia, soared from 8,425 in 1860 to 101,109 in 1870 and 1,301,826 in 1890. Wisconsin, Iowa, Illinois, and the Dakotas showed similar rises. But the bitter winter of 1886–1887 and the successive years of failing wheat crops slowed the incoming pace. Beginning with the early 1890s Scandinavians responded to the industrial opportunities in the Northeast and the Middle Atlantic States and the lumber camps and sawmills of the Pacific Northwest. The influx of Scandinavians and others into the state of Washington, for example, reached such proportions that the state population jumped from 75,000 in 1880 to over a million in 1910. Every census after 1910 shows more than 60 percent of the Swedish-born and their children living in urban areas. In 1917 Chicago had the largest number of Swedes and Norwegians in the world next to Stockholm and Oslo, respectively, and 13 years later the federal census found a sizable Norwegian population comfortably established in a middle-class neighborhood in Brooklyn.

Other nineteenth-century newcomers went to both urban and rural areas. The French Canadians had established small communities in Winooski, Vermont, and Woonsocket, Rhode Island, as early as 1814 and 1815, respectively, and later settlements in Madawaska and Burlington, Vermont, before 1850. By the end of the nineteenth century they constituted one of the major minorities in New England and much smaller ones in the cities of northern New York, Michigan, Illinois, and Wisconsin. The Welsh who came to America headed for the mining camps in Pennsylvania and Ohio, while the Dutch, who went to Michigan in 1846, had small colonies there as well as in New York, while a few others established themselves in Arizona and Wyoming. Even the South—whose officials and some businessmen desired northern and western Europeans to fill the labor ranks (white Southerners commonly considered blacks unsuitable for any work other than farm and domestic service) but whose population in general did not want intruders— received contingents of foreigners. Swedes went to Thornsby, Arkansas; Danes farmed in Mississippi; Italians worked in Louisiana, Mississippi, and Tennessee; the Irish bolstered the population of several Southern cities; a Slavic community developed near Petersburg, Virginia; and some Chinese planted themselves in Mississippi.

Wherever they went and whoever they were, the immigrants lived and worked under conditions that were far from idyllic. Mass immigration resulted in new social problems for American communities, especially in the congested urban areas like New York City and Chicago. Many immigrants were either unemployed or underemployed, and disease and poverty were common. Inexperienced with such problems, Americans proved unable to cope with them except superficially.

Immigrants generally found work easily in the United States but often in unskilled jobs. In cities like New York, Boston, and Chicago immigrants comprised the bulk of the unskilled laborers, porters, street cleaners, bartenders, waiters, draymen, cabmen, carmen, livery workers, and domestics. The Irish could be found as stevedores on docks at every major port in the country. In New England they replaced American girls in the mills and later stepped aside for the French Canadians. Two-thirds of the domestics in Boston by 1860 were Irish, usually young women, and the census of that year also noted that they held most of the city's common laboring jobs. Germans in New York held menial positions but also qualified as tailors and skilled craftsmen in the furniture, cabinetmaking, and bookbinding firms; in Cincinnati they were dominant in the stove and musical-instrument industries. Those Norwegians who did not farm worked in ᵗhe iron mines and lumber camps in Michigan, and sawmills and fisheries in the Pacific Northwest, and at other industrial tasks in places as diverse as Tacoma, Cleveland, and Brooklyn. Workers were always needed until the completion of the canals and railroads, and strapping Irishmen won a reputation for talent and skill in these construction industries. Irish laborers built the Illinois Central Railroad before the company employed German hands. The Union Pacific used Mexicans, Germans, Chinese, and Irish to get its lines going. Scandinavian, Irish, and German women had no qualms about serving as domestics, but French Canadians shunned personal service for factory work. The mainstay of the late nineteenth-century New England textile mills, the French-Canadian family, insisted that all its members be employed at the same establishment. They put little premium on education and thought that children as well as adults should contribute to the family coffers. One overseer in a textile mill recalled telling a French-Canadian family that the law prohibited the hiring of children under ten, "and the next day they were all ten." In the West the Chinese were forced to accept the menial jobs that whites shunned in mines, domestic service, and on the farms. Chinese also opened restaurants and laundries, and they comprised half of California's agricultural workers by 1884.

Some immigrants were excluded from unions while others, unfamiliar with American laboring practices and the advantages of unions, worked as scabs and strikebreakers. Chinese laborers showed little regard for the white man's union, and when white miners struck in 1875, the Union Pacific brought 125 Chinese to mine in Rock Springs, Wyoming. Ten years later a similar problem resulted in the further importation of Chinese workers, who refused to join the Knights of Labor. This no doubt precipitated the September 1885 massacre in Rock Springs, where whites killed 28 Chinese laborers, wounded 15 others, and chased several hundred out of town.

The conditions under which Americans and immigrants labored were often appalling. Since American wages were much higher than those in Europe and Asia, emigrants did not realize that there could be economic hardships in the United States. In Sweden farm hands earned $33.50 *a year,* plus room and board. It is no wonder, therefore, that a salary of $40 *a month* in the Pennsylvania coal mines, $1.25 to $2.00 a day on a railroad construction gang, or $200 a year as an American farm hand would be appealing. Not until they reached the United States and had to cope with the realities of urban squalor or rural depression did the emigrants realize that the American laborer did not lead a princely existence.

In the Midwest during the boom times after the Civil War, farm income was relatively high. Wheat sold for $1.50 a bushel, and hard work seemed to ensure prosperity. But wheat prices fell on the world market in the 1890s to 50 cents a bushel. Countless thousands were ruined. There is no doubt that the failure of wheat crops in places like Kansas, Nebraska, Minnesota, and the Dakotas contributed to the decline in migration to those areas in the late 1880s and early 1890s.

Employees in industrial enterprises fared just as badly as those on the farm. In the nineteenth century there was usually a chronic labor shortage even though at times a city like Boston had more people than jobs. But the pay in most occupations failed to sustain even a modest standard of living. In 1851 *The New York Times* and the New York *Tribune* published estimated budgets for a family of five. The first came to about $600 a year, the second to $539. Yet when one looks at the wage scales, it is apparent that most employees' yearly incomes fell far short of this figure. A skilled tailor might earn $6 to $9 a week but did not work a 52-week year. Cabinetmakers earned $5 a week, and common laborers took home $20 to $30 a month. A journeyman dressmaker earned $1.25 to $1.50 for a 14- to 16-hour day. In Boston, in 1830, when the annual cost of living was $440, the average workingman's salary was $230; in 1864, when the cost of living rose to $810, the average unskilled laborer earned only $465. Real wages increased in the decades after the Civil War, but many immigrant families earned only a few hundred dollars a year and had to struggle to maintain even a modest standard of living.

With such low wages and yearly incomes one can understand why so many immigrants, and many native Americans, lived in quite humble and often outright squalid dwellings. The typical Norwegian in the upper Midwest built a log cabin 12 feet by 12 or 14 feet, with a height of from 7 to 14 feet, for himself and his family. The early Dutch pioneers of Michigan lived under bedsheets framed on hemlock branches, with a cooking pot outside. When they earned enough to build a more commodious abode, several families shared a one-room log cabin.

Urban enclaves were little better. In small cities like Fall River and Holyoke, Massachusetts, French Canadians crowded into dark, dank, and rat-infested tenements, which one chronicler pronounced "worse than the old slave quarters." Housing in most of the major

Table 2–2. The Urban Immigrant: 1870 Populations of the Irish, the Germans, and the English in American Cities

Name of City	Total Population	Irish	Germans	English
1. New York, N. Y.	942,292	202,000	151,203	24,408
2. Philadelphia, Pa.	674,022	96,698	50,746	22,034
3. Brooklyn, N.Y.	376,099	73,985	36,769	18,832
4. St. Louis, Mo.	310,864	32,239	59,040	5,366
5. Chicago, Ill.	298,977	40,000	52,316	10,026
6. Baltimore, Md.	267,354	15,223	35,276	2,138
7. Boston, Mass.	250,526	56,900	5,606	6,000
8. Cincinnati, Ohio	216,239	18,624	49,446	3,524
9. New Orleans, La.	191,418	14,693	15,224	2,005
10. San Francisco, Cal.	149,473	25,864	13,602	5,166
11. Buffalo, N. Y.	117,714	11,264	22,249	3,558
12. Washington, D. C.	109,200	6,948	4,131	1,231
13. Newark, N.J.	105,059	12,481	15,873	4,040
14. Louisville, Ky.	100,753	7,626	14,380	930
15. Cleveland, Ohio	92,829	9,964	15,855	4,530
16. Pittsburgh, Pa.	86,076	13,119	8,703	2,838
17. Jersey City, N. J.	82,546	17,665	7,151	4,005
18. Detroit, Mich.	79,577	6,970	12,647	3,282
19. Milwaukee, Wis.	71,440	3,784	22,600	1,395
20. Albany, N. Y.	69,422	13,276	5,168	1,572
21. Providence, R. I.	68,904	12,085	596	2,426
22. Rochester, N. Y.	62,386	6,078	7,730	2,530
23. Alleghany, Pa.	53,180	4,034	7,665	1,112
24. Richmond, Va.	51,038	1,239	1,621	289
25. New Haven, Conn.	50,840	9,601	2,423	1,087
26. Charleston, S. C.	48,956	2,180	1,826	234
27. Indianapolis, Ind.	48,244	3,321	5,286	697
28. Troy, N. Y.	46,465	10,877	1,174	1,575
29. Syracuse, N. Y.	43,051	5,172	5,062	1,345
30. Worcester, Mass.	41,105	8,389	325	893
31. Lowell, Mass.	40,928	9,103	34	1,697
32. Memphis, Tenn.	40,226	2,987	1,768	589
33. Cambridge, Mass.	39,634	7,180	482	1,043
34. Hartford, Conn.	37,180	7,438	1,458	787
35. Scranton, Pa.	35,092	6,491	3,056	1,444
36. Reading, Pa.	33,930	547	2,648	305
37. Paterson, N. J.	33,600	5,124	1,429	3,347
38. Kansas City, Mo.	32,260	2,869	1,884	709
39. Mobile, Ala.	32,034	2,000	843	386
40. Toledo, Ohio	31,584	3,032	5,341	694
41. Portland, Me.	31,413	3,900	82	557
42. Columbus, Ohio	31,274	1,845	3,982	504

Table 2–2. The Urban Immigrant: 1870 Populations of the Irish, the Germans, and the English in American Cities (continued)

Name of City	Total Population	Irish	Germans	English
43. Wilmington, Del.	30,841	3,503	684	613
44. Dayton, Ohio	30,473	1,326	4,962	394
45. Lawrence, Mass.	28,921	7,457	467	2,456
46. Utica, N. Y.	28,804	3,496	2,822	1,352
47. Charlestown, Mass.	28,323	4,803	216	488
48. Savannah, Ga.	28,235	2,197	787	251
49. Lynn, Mass.	28,233	3,232	17	330
50. Fall River, Mass.	26,766	5,572	37	4,042

SOURCE: U.S. Census, 1870.

urban centers was also appalling. In Boston the Irish resided in "crammed hovels . . . without furniture and with patches of dirty straw" or in damp cellars that flowed with raw sewage after heavy rains or in reconverted factory lofts with leaking roofs, broken windows and no running water. Historian Oscar Handlin, who vividly chronicled their experiences, tells us that in winter the Boston Irish often remained in bed all day to protect themselves from the cold or "huddled together like brutes, without regard to sex, or age, or sense of decency. . . ."

Dwellings in New York were no better. In the middle of the century 18,000 people lived in cellars without light, air, or drainage, and even those who lived above them had to use outdoor, and often malfunctioning, privies—winter and summer. Overcrowding was proverbial; half a million people lived in 16,000 dilapidated tenements. The Irish often grouped five or six families in a single flat. Three quarters of the city had no sewers; garbage and horse droppings littered ghetto streets.

The appalling overcrowding of immigrants and lack of proper sanitation led to continual bouts with disease. The newcomers frequently contracted such ailments as consumption, cancer, pneumonia, diarrhea, and bronchitis. They were also victims of periodic epidemics of typhoid, typhus, and cholera, which spread through the slums like forest fires in a parched woods. Cities having the largest immigrant populations—New York, St. Louis, Cincinnati, and New Orleans—suffered the most from these outbreaks. In 1851 a cholera epidemic hit Chicago, and in one three-block section where 332 Scandinavians (mostly Norwegians) lived, *everyone* died from the disease. Hospitals and lunatic asylums housed disproportionately high numbers of newcomers. In New York in the 1850s the Irish comprised 85 percent of the foreign-born admitted to Bellevue Hospital and most of the admissions to Blackwell's Island, the city's asylum for mental patients.

Many immigrants, try as they might, could not avoid the almshouses. Those forced to accept charity also had to tolerate the sanctimonious declaration that they were merely "the indolent, the aged, and infirm who can earn their subsistence nowhere, [but must] become a burden, and often because of their vices, a nuisance to the community." The foreign-born outnumbered the native-born in the various poorhouses of the nation in 1850, and in some states, like New York, the ratio was greater than 2 to 1. And the problem became worse as greater numbers of immigrants arrived.

Among the most serious difficulties encountered by the immigrants was American intolerance for ethnic differences. Each immigrant group experienced hostility in countless ways. The best jobs were often closed to them, and employers often posted signs like "Irish Need Not Apply." Institutions dealing with the foreign-born, like almshouses, hospital dispensaries, and employment bureaus, treated their clients with "a ridiculous, often brutal disdain." Hardly any minority escaped the barbs of the prejudiced. The Germans received abuse from several sides. Temperance advocates did not like their making merry, drinking beer, and ignoring the Puritan Sabbath. Conservative Americans distrusted radical and reform-minded German exiles from the abortive revolutions of 1848 who supported the abolition of slavery, women's rights, and other liberal causes in America.

Economics in part explains ethnic intolerance. The increase in immigration, especially of many poverty-stricken refugees from Ireland, aroused American fears of having too many poor people. And large numbers of unskilled laborers, it was argued, would also depress wages and the American standard of living. Americans also deplored what they considered the immigrants' striking personal deficiencies. A Massachusetts Bureau of Labor Statistics report in the 1880s censured the French Canadians for their lack of "moral character, their lack of respect for American institutions, their failure to become naturalized, and their opposition to education."

Before the Civil War the most important source of conflict be-

tween native-born and immigrant was religion. More precisely, the
key battles were fought over American objections to Irish Catholics.
The underlying issue revolved around the American belief that
Roman Catholicism and American institutions, which were based
on Protestant concepts, were incompatible. In this view if Catholics "took over" America, the Pope in Rome would rule and
religious and political liberty would be destroyed. Samuel F. B.
Morse, the inventor of the telegraph, believed that there was a
Catholic plot to destroy the United States. He held that the Church
was sending Jesuit-controlled immigrants to America. Writing in
1835 he asked his countrymen not to be any longer "deceived by the
pensioned Jesuits, who have surrounded your press, are now using
it all over the country to stifle the cries of danger, and lull your fears
by attributing your alarm to a false cause. . . . To your posts! . . .
Fly to protect the vulnerable places of your Constitution and Laws.
Place your guards; you will need them, and quickly too. —And first,
shut your gates."

Morse was not the only impassioned enemy of Catholicism.
Militant Protestants published sensational exposés of the Church.
The most famous of the anti-Catholic accounts was Maria Monk's
Awful Disclosures of the Hotel Dieu Nunnery of Montreal, published in 1836. This gothic horror tale was frequently reprinted and
sold several hundred thousand copies. According to her inflamma-
tory story, the author was compelled to live in sin with priests in
the nunnery and witnessed the execution of nuns for refusing to sub-
mit to the carnal lusts of priests. She even insisted that babies were
strangled and buried in the basement of the Hotel Dieu Nunnery.
Such yarns created inevitable controversy. On the one hand, her
work was cited by anti-Catholics as proof of their worst fears, and,
on the other hand, indignant Catholics and skeptical Protestants
denounced the book as a fraud. Investigations turned up no evidence
to support her charges, and Maria Monk was personally discredited as a prostitute. Nevertheless, many believed her story,
and the book continued to inflame the passions of the anti-Catholic crusade. Her success encouraged others to publish similar hair-
raising stories, and she herself added to the literature by writing
Further Disclosures, also about the Hotel Dieu.

These accounts fanned the passions of the day and contributed
to violence. In August of 1834 an angry mob burned the Ursuline
Convent outside of Boston. Nativist violence occurred in other places

in ante-bellum America, including a riot in Philadelphia in the summer of 1844. Most conflicts did not lead to violence but involved controversies over control of church property, religious teaching in the schools, and the general issues of separation of church and state.

Not satisfied with exposés and agitation, the nativists turned to state and national politics for weapons against the detested Catholics. A few nativist political organizations and parties existed prior to 1850, but the major nativist party was the Know-Nothing or American party of the 1850s. A large secret organization, the Know-Nothings suffered from a number of sectional disagreements and eventually fell apart as a national movement, but at its peak it was held together by a suspicion of the Roman Catholic Church. In 1854 the party scored victories at the polls, won control of several state governments, and sent dozens of congressmen to Washington, D.C. The major strength of the Know-Nothings lay in the Northeast and the border states. Once in office the nativists proposed a number of bills to restrict the franchise and to make naturalization a longer process. They also established legislative committees to investigate the alleged misconduct in Catholic institutions. Many Know-Nothings who took Maria Monk seriously were convinced that nuns were being held as virtual prisoners in convents against their wills, and they petitioned state governments to free these women.

The proposals and investigations produced few results, however, nor did the agitation lead to immigration restriction. The movement failed, in part, because the party was fragmented. It also failed, in part, because discussions concerning the morality and extension of slavery consumed American political attention in the late 1850s. But most important, despite fear of the Catholics and other alleged evils of immigration, was the fact that Americans welcomed immigrants because they were needed to help the nation expand and develop economically.

Yet, native hostility did exist, and it is understandable why the newcomers clustered together. Even without the antagonisms heaped upon them they would probably have settled in ethnic enclaves; but if they had been accepted warmly, their children and grandchildren might have moved into the mainstream of American life at a much faster pace. Naturally, the foreigners clung to their languages and their churches. They also set up newspapers to interpret the American scene for them, and some groups, especially the Irish but also many Germans and Scandinavians, established parochial schools to preserve traditions that most Americans frowned upon. The French Canadians feared that the loss of their particular language would mean loss of faith, which to them meant absolute loss of identity. For the Irish, language presented hardly any problem, but their church claimed their staunchest allegiance. To them nothing seemed as important as keeping the faith.

Germans were not as staunch churchgoers as the Irish, nor did religion mean as much to most of them. But they were regarded as the most clannish of the foreigners, and they did little to alter this impression. Great efforts were made to maintain the Old World culture, and women especially were admonished "that they must seek to preserve the German spirit in their children." A Texas grandmother, who had come to this country as a girl of ten in 1846, published her memoirs, *Was Grossmutter Erzählt* (1915), in her native tongue and reminded readers that "German family life stands for the preservation of an ideal culture, which can only continue to exert its influence if respected from generation to generation." Most German Americans obviously felt the same way, for at the beginning of the twentieth century it was still quite rare to find Midwestern Germans who had chosen mates from other ethnic groups, and on the eve of World War I 70 percent of the Lutheran churches in St. Louis still conducted their services in German.

The intense concern for preserving the culture of the *Vaterland* also led to vigorous organizational activities. The German Americans maintained the most extensive number of newspapers, fraternal organizations, gymnastic and cultural societies, choral and athletic groups, and benevolent organizations. It was proverbial that the Germans loved their beer, their convivial picnics, and their pleasure-filled Sundays. Yet the coming of World War I marked the decline of the hyphenated German-American culture. The country then demanded 100 percent loyalty and denounced everything and everyone that smacked of "the Hun." Though many resented the pressures upon them, German Americans made a strong effort to conform to the dominant customs and thereby weakened their own heritage.

The Scandinavians, who were mostly Lutheran, were more devout and more strait-laced than the Germans. No one caricatured them as jolly or frolicsome. Their faith, a stern one that frowned upon drinking, dancing, and levity, also provided a complete philosophy of life stressing piety along with the work ethic. This influence was so pervasive and persistent that in 1934 fully two-thirds of all the Protestant church members in Minnesota, Wisconsin, and the Dakotas still belonged to the Lutheran Church.

The security derived from the family, ethnic neighborhood, school, church, society, and newspaper hastened the day when the immigrant child or grandchild could stand securely on his own and move into the mainstream of American life. Having been nurtured in relative security, he had the strength to meet head-on new challenges of becoming Americanized. He knew, however, that the customs that provided a secure ground for his parents or grandparents would not suffice for him in the United States.

Chapter 3

The New Immigrants

As the nineteenth century progressed, industrialization moved southward and eastward in Europe. Uprooted peoples left their farms and small villages, moved into towns and cities, crossed national boundaries, and traversed the oceans. The movement was world-wide, and millions of Europeans dispersed themselves throughout Europe and the Western Hemisphere. Cities like Warsaw, Berlin, Vienna, Naples, and London were as much inundated by the newcomers as were New York, Chicago, and Philadelphia in the United States. Germany, France, Brazil, Argentina, and Great Britain received hundreds of thousands of immigrants. However, the United States with its higher standard of living and reputation for being a land of golden opportunity attracted the bulk of the migrants. Between 1880, when the southern and eastern Europeans began making their significance felt on American immigration statistics, and 1930, when the combination of immigration restriction laws and a major depression put barriers in their way, the United States received a total of 27 million immigrants.

After 1890 newcomers from northern and western Europe continued coming to American shores; but they did not have the same impact in either numbers or percentages that the immigrants from southern and eastern Europe had. In the nineteenth century, for example, 1882 was the peak year of immigration. Of the total of 788,992 immigrants of that year 250,630 were from Germany, and only 32,159 were from Italy, 27,935 from the Austro-Hungarian Empire, and 16,918 from Russia and the Baltic countries. In 1907, the peak year for the twentieth-century migration, of the 1,285,349 recorded entrants only 37,807 came from Germany, while 285,731 came from Italy, 338,452 from the Austro-Hungarian

Empire, and 258,943 from Russia and the Baltic States. These southern and eastern Europeans, the so-called new immigrants, were trying to escape from economic strangulation and despair just as the Germans, Irish, and Scandinavians had before them. The southern Italians, especially, fled horrendous conditions. Unemployment, high birth rates, overpopulation, cholera and malaria epidemics were only some of the problems besetting these people. Many of the Italian peasants lived in houses of straw or even in rock caves and abandoned Greek tombs. Often, one-room shacks housed people and livestock together. An agricultural laborer earned from 8 to 32 cents a day in Sicily but rarely found enough work during the year. Furthermore, while the population in Italy increased by 25 percent from 1871 to 1905, the economy slackened. Wheat, citrus fruits, and wine, commodities that were the mainsprings of the Italian rural economy, declined drastically in price on the world market. The resulting increase in poverty was so great that some Italian arrivals in the United States declared afterward, "We would have eaten each other had we stayed."

Some northern Italians had left the country earlier in the nineteenth century. After national unification in 1859, though, relaxed emigration restrictions and expanded steamship advertising combined with a depressed economy to induce many southern as well as northern Italian men and boys and a few women to seek their fortunes in the New World. Many went to Brazil and Argentina, but depressions in those countries in the 1890s directed the traffic to the United States. The comparative prosperity and opportunities here, which were communicated by mail and returning immigrants, finally resulted in a deluge of emigrants, many of whom left Italy through Naples. From 1881 to 1910 more than 3 million Italians sailed for the United States.

Jews ranked second to the Italians among the new arrivals. In the late nineteenth and early twentieth centuries over 2 million of them left eastern Europe, more than 70 percent of these coming from Russia. Over 90 percent of the Jews headed for the United States, while the minority removed themselves to cities in central and western Europe, Canada, and Latin America. If others were victimized by a changing agricultural economy, the Jews were aliens in the land of their birth. Russian laws, with few exceptions, restricted them to life in the pale of settlement (mostly in eastern Poland and western Russia), curtailed their educational and occu-

pational opportunities, and conscripted Jewish youths at the age
of 12 for 31 years of military service. Things were made still worse
by violence. The assassination of Czar Alexander II in 1881 set
off a wave of government-condoned pogroms—brutal beatings, kill-
ings, and lootings—which lasted for about 30 years. Jews never
knew where or when the terror would strike next. A particularly
devastating pogrom that occurred in the city of Kishineff in 1903
involved 2,750 families; 47 people were killed and 424 were
wounded; many Jewish homes were burned, and Jewish shops
were pillaged. The massacre received world-wide attention and also
resulted in a vastly increased number of Jews emigrating from
Russia. As a consequence of these East European migrations, the
Jewish population in the United States soared from about 250,000
(mostly of German descent) in 1877 to past the 4-million mark in
1927.

The Slavic groups—which included Russians, Ruthenians
(Ukrainians), Slovaks, Slovenes, Poles, Croatians, Serbs, and Bul-
garians—together accounted for about one-fourth of the new arrivals in the United States. Each of these ethnic groups had a dis-
tinctive language, customs, and historical experience, but most
dispersed themselves throughout the country and either set up
separate enclaves or else blended in with other Slavic groups. Aside
from the Poles and Czechs, many were mistakenly identified in the
census tracts or lumped together as Slavs and otherwise ignored.

The Poles, the largest of the Slavic groups, were counted separately after 1899, and as a result we know that after the Italians
and the Jews they were the third largest element among early
twentieth-century immigrants. Well over 1 million Poles arrived
before World War I; their coming can be attributed to the acute
poverty in territory controlled by Russia and the suppression of
Polish culture and nationalism in the sections of Poland under
German domination.

In addition to these groups the United States received about a
million Magyars from Hungary, perhaps 300,000 Greeks, 146,000
Portuguese, 70,000 or 80,000 Armenians, and thousands of Syrians
escaping from Turkish tyranny; about 90,000 Japanese came from
the Orient and Hawaii. World War I temporarily interrupted the
major flow, but in the 1920s another 350,000 Italians, 300,000
Scots (more than the entire colonial migration from Scotland),
almost 500,000 legally accounted for Mexicans (as many or more

crossed the border illegally), and about 200,000 Germans continued streaming into this country.

The majority of the immigrants, old and new, consisted of males who came without families; among the Irish, though, females made up a majority. Of the European immigrants 78 percent of the Italians and 95 percent of the Greeks were males, while many Jews came as families. From Asia the Japanese immigrants, like the Chinese before them, were overwhelmingly male. Although many men often sent for their wives and children afterward, others hoped to make their fame and fortune and return. Few made fortunes, but many did return.

Intelligent estimates of how many foreigners returned to their native countries range from a high of nearly 90 percent for the Balkan peoples to a low of 5 percent for the Jews. We do know that in the period between 1908 and 1914 immigration officials recorded 6,709,357 arrivals and 2,063,767 departures. During these years, more than half of the Hungarians, Italians, Croatians, and Slovenes returned to Europe. For the most part returnees included a high percentage of single men. A number of Italian men annually migrated to Italy in the fall, returning to the United States the next spring. The availability of jobs determined their movement. During the winter months, many Italians in railroad, construction, and mining work saw no point in remaining unemployed in the United States. From 1908 through 1916, 1,215,998 Italians left the United States. This back-and-forth migration, however, virtually ceased by the mid-1920s after the quota system went into effect.

Eighty percent of the new immigrants settled in the northeastern section of the United States, roughly from Washington, D.C., in the southeast, St. Louis in the southwest, the Mississippi River, Canada, and the Atlantic Ocean. Two-thirds of all the immigrants could be found in New York, New England, Pennsylvania, and New Jersey, while sizable numbers also gravitated toward states like Illinois and Ohio. Relatively few went to the South.

The major cities, especially New York and Chicago, proved particularly attractive because of the jobs available, because of their location as major transportation depots, and because they were inhabited by compatriots who could help the immigrants adjust to the New World situation. A majority of the Italians and Jews remained in New York. Other groups also found city life desirable. According to the census records of 1910, about three quarters of the population of New York, Chicago, Detroit, Cleveland, and Boston were made up of immigrants and their children. Foreign enclaves also dominated cities like Philadelphia, Milwaukee, Buffalo, Baltimore, Pittsburgh, and Providence. In 1916, 72 percent of San Francisco's population spoke a foreign language.

Although some habitats naturally had more to offer than others, no *area* of the United States escaped the immigrants' attention or proved totally unsuitable to all groups. Thus one could find—even today—Italians in Louisiana, Michigan, and Colorado, Hungarians and Greeks in Florida, Slavs in Virginia, Mexicans in Illinois, Irish in Montana, Armenians in Massachusetts and California, Basques in Idaho and Oregon, Russians in North Dakota, and Jews in Arizona and New Mexico. Certainly, they constituted minorities in these states, but it is significant that so many places in the United States afforded opportunities to the venturesome.

The immigrants came with high hopes, unprepared for the coolness with which so many Americans received them. Like others before them, the new immigrants were stereotyped as representatives of some kind of lower species. None of the newer groups escaped American contempt. Greeks were physically attacked in Omaha, Nebraska, and they were forced out of Mountain View, Idaho. A New Englander, observing some Poles weeding rows of onions, commented: "Animals, they work under the sun and in the dirt; with stolid, stupid faces." On the West Coast the people of San Francisco created an international incident by segregating fewer than 100 Japanese students in the city's schools.

Italians, however, who outnumbered all other twentieth-century European immigrants, were one of the most despised groups. Old stock Americans called them wops, dagos, and guineas and referred to them as the "Chinese of Europe" and as being "just as bad as the Negroes." In the South some Italians were forced to attend all-black schools, and in both the North and the South they were victimized by brutality. In 1875 *The New York Times* thought it "perhaps hopeless to think of civilizing them, or keeping them in order, except by the arm of the law." Other newspapers proclaimed that Italians were criminal by nature, and a supposedly intelligent and sympathetic observer wrote that Italians "are as a race simple-minded and often grossly ignorant." The University of Wisconsin sociologist E. A. Ross, one of the Progressive era's most outspoken bigots, explained that crime in Italy had declined significantly since the migrations began "because all the criminals are here." Americans were fortified in their beliefs about southern Italians because many northern Italians, who had arrived here decades earlier, also regarded their compatriots from the south as "an army of barbarians encamped among us."

Jews experienced similar problems. In colonial America Jews had not been able to vote, and these restrictions lasted, in some states, until well into the nineteenth century. Not until New Hampshire removed its barriers in 1877 did American Jews have the franchise in every state. Even where there were no Jews, prejudice and misconceptions were widespread. On the stage the Jew almost always appeared as a scoundrel. To have portrayed him in a sympathetic or admirable vein, one scholar tells us, "would have been in defiance of the centuries-old tradition that in the drama the Jew must be the villain or the object of derision."

When the East European Jews arrived, they were often scorned, even by the German Jews. The German Jews who had arrived in the mid-nineteenth century did not want Russian, Galician, and Rumanian Jews in their midst. German Jews had achieved considerable success in the United States, and had absorbed the nation's values, and many had even refurbished their religious practices, bringing them more into line with Protestantism. The stampede of East European Jews with their long beards, peculiar clothing, and staunch devotion to an orthodox faith that seemed strange to many Americans threatened members of the established Jewish community. They envisioned, correctly, an increase in anti-Semitic feeling, which would affect their hard-won respectability. Their views were most specifically stated in an 1894 issue of the *Hebrew Standard*: "The thoroughly acclimated American Jew ... has no religious, social or intellectual sympathies with the East European Jew. He is closer to the Christian sentiment around him than to the Judaism of these miserable darkened Hebrews." But the American Jews could do nothing to stem the East European tide, nor could they stop other Americans from lumping all Jews together. Once they recognized these facts, they reversed their position and did what they could to help the newcomers adjust to life in America.

Although the German Jews eventually reconciled themselves to having their brethren from eastern Europe in the United States, other Americans did not. Beginning in the 1870s the latent, or often privately uttered, anti-Semitism emerged into the open and struck first at those Jews who were the most Americanized. The New York Bar Association blackballed a Jew who applied for membership in 1877; a City College of New York fraternity did the same thing a year later; and a major resort hotel in Saratoga Springs, New York, barred a long-time guest, Joseph Seligman, one of New York City's leading bankers. Thereafter, clubs, resorts, and private schools increasingly turned away Jewish patrons. Hostility toward Jews knew no geographical bounds. In the 1890s Jewish merchants in the South had their stores wrecked and were harassed by threats to leave town. In a New Jersey mill town several days of rioting resulted after a local firm hired 14 Jews. By the Progressive era, open discrimination prevailed in housing and employment. Hotels displayed signs proclaiming "No Jews Allowed," and job advertisements specified "Christians Only."

No amount of prejudice or hostility toward the newcomers, however, prevented employers from putting the greenhorns to work. The industrial sections of the country needed cheap labor continually, and the numerous foreigners provided the necessary hands. Older immigrants and native-born workers would not tolerate conditions the immigrants had to accept, and so toward the end of the nineteenth century Slavs and Italians replaced British, Irish, and Germans in the Pennsylvania coal mines; Portuguese, Greeks, Syrians, Armenians, and Italians worked alongside French Canadians in the New England textile mills; East European Jews took over the jobs formerly held by the Irish and Germans in New York City's garment factories, and the Japanese on the West Coast did the agricultural and menial tasks that had formerly been the province of the Chinese.

Because immigrants felt more comfortable working and living among their friends and relatives ethnic groups concentrated in particular industries and occupations. The Slavic groups located in the mining and industrial regions of western Pennsylvania, Ohio, Illinois, Michigan, and New York. They also provided the bulk of the labor in Chicago's slaughterhouses and Pennsylvania's steel mills, where they were considered desirable because of "their habit of silent submission, their amenability to discipline and their willingness to work long hours and overtime without a murmur." Or, as the Pittsburgh *Leader* bluntly put it, the East European immigrant made "a better slave than the American." About one-third of the Poles also went into farming in the Northeast and the Midwest. They did truck gardening in Long Island, cultivated tobacco, onions, and asparagus in the Connecticut Valley, and planted corn and wheat in the north central Midwest.

The Greeks avoided farming but went into industry or operated small businesses of their own. One survey at the beginning of the twentieth century found that about 30,000 to 40,000 of the 150,000 Greeks in the United States were laborers in factories or on railroad construction gangs. But others peddled fruit and vegetables, maintained shoeshine and ice-cream parlors, flower shops, restaurants, or confectionaries. The association of Greeks with candy and food was proverbial. Chicago became the center of their sweets trade, and in 1904 a Greek newspaperman observed that "practically every busy corner in Chicago is occupied by a Greek candy store." After World War II the Greeks still maintained 350 to 450 confectionary shops and eight to ten candy manufacturers in the Windy City. Most Americans still connect the Greeks with restaurants, and for good reason. Almost every major American city boasts of its fine Greek eating establishments, a tradition that goes back more than half a century. After World War I, for example, estimates were that the Greeks owned 564 restaurants in San Francisco alone.

The Italians settled everywhere and entered almost every occupation, or so it seems at first glance. They built subways in New York, manufactured cigars in Florida, and made wine in California. In Chicago they manned the stockyards, and in San Francisco they caught fish. They comprised a large number of New England's textile workers and were second only to the Jews in New York's garment trades. They provided gang labor on railroads and construction projects and worked underground in the bituminous fields of Illinois, Kansas, and Oklahoma, the iron mines of Michigan and Minnesota, and the copper and silver mines of Colorado, Arizona, and Montana. In 1894 they constituted all but 1 of New York City's 474 foreign-born bootblacks, and in 1897 they made up 75 percent of the city's construction workers. They moved into major sanitation departments in New York, Chicago, and Philadelphia. In 1911 a federal commission found that they accounted for the largest number of common laborers of any ethnic group in America.

But the Italians also yearned for the security of their own businesses, and, as soon as they were able, they bought pushcarts or opened small stores. In New York City they dominated the fruit business in all its phases from produce market to retail outlet. They opened shoe-repair shops, restaurants, groceries, and bakeries. Some manufactured spaghetti, while others made candy. Many cut hair, and by 1910 more than half the barbers in New York City were Italian.

Unlike the Italians who left Europe for the most part illiterate and unskilled 67 percent of the Jewish males who arrived in the early part of the twentieth century were classified as skilled workers. This figure compared with an average of 20 percent for all other male immigrants. Most of the Jews utilized their craftsmanship in New York's garment trades, which contained half of all the city's Jewish workers and two-thirds of its Jewish wage earners. On the eve of World War I, in fact, Jews comprised 70 percent of all workers in New York's clothing industry. Other Jewish workers found positions in cigar factories and distilleries, as printers and bookbinders, and as skilled carpenters. For the unskilled a peddler's pushcart often opened the path to settled retail trade throughout the country, while the enormous numbers of Jews, with their special dietary needs, gave rise to the establishment of kosher butchers, grocers, and neighborhood candy stores, which also sold soda water, newspapers, stationery, tobacco, and sundries. The Jews also found opportunities for themselves in music and the theater, and in the early decades of the twentieth century they made up half the actors, popular songwriters, and song publishers in New York City.

Wherever the newcomers labored, employers sapped them of their energies before replacing them with fresh recruits. Industrial accidents were common. The famous Triangle shirtwaist factory fire of New York City in 1911 took the lives of 146, mainly young women. One fireman told of the horror of the girls leaping to their deaths: "They hit the pavement just like hail. We could hear the thuds faster than we could see the bodies fall." Construction and railroad workers also frequently met with fatal injuries, as did newcomers in the Pittsburgh steel mills. Even where workers were fortunate to escape fatal injuries, working conditions often ensured irreparable damage to health. In Riverside, California, Armenian cement makers inhaled dust and poisonous gases emitted in the large, overheated grinding rooms. In Chicago Greek teenagers slaved in shoeshine parlors from six A.M. through nine P.M. Afterward the boys had to clean the stores before being allowed to return to barrackslike dwellings for a supper of stale bread and watery soup. The yearly earnings of a shoeshine boy were from $160 to $180. A

Hungarian immigrant complained about his experiences in a Pitts-burgh steel mill: "Wherever the heat is most insupportable, the flames most scorching, the smoke and soot most choking, there we are certain to find compatriots bent and wasted with toil." In New York home sweatshops whole families bent over coats and suits with their sewing needles.

In the labor camps, where many immigrant men came to work, conditions were as bad, or even worse, than in the cities. Armed guards patrolled isolated labor camps in Georgia and West Vir-ginia, and beatings with iron bars and gun butts kept the men at their jobs. When a Hungarian immigrant tried to escape from a Georgian lumber camp, his bosses went after him with trained dogs. When they caught him, he was horsewhipped and then tied to the buggy for the return trip. Peonage, though illegal of course, was widely practiced. Eventually, charges were brought against this particular lumber camp and the owners had to stand trial. As the Hungarian peon recalled, a peculiar kind of justice was enacted. "Of all things that mixed my thinking in America," the Hungarian later wrote, "nothing was so strange as to find that the bosses who were indicted for holding us in peonage could go out free on bail, while we, the laborers, who had been flogged and beaten and robbed, should be kept in jail because we had neither money nor friends." In a West Virginia labor camp Italian workers slept in wooden boxcars where "the dirt of two years covered the mattresses. Roaches and bedbugs livened the walls and held undis-puted sway of the beds and their immediate surroundings. . . . All doors were closed at night. No windows, no air. Nothing seemed to have been left undone to reduce human beings to animals." The workday for these men lasted from five A.M. to four P.M. with an hour off for lunch. They were never given morning breaks be-cause the padrone who controlled them resisted: "The beasts must not be given a rest. Otherwise they will step over me."

Not all oppressors were native Americans. Greek and Italian padrones, or labor agents, exercised great control over the immi-grants. The padrones who had come to the United States earlier, spoke English and arranged jobs and found living accommodations for their later-arriving compatriots. Men and boys were sent off to railroad and construction gangs, lumber camps, and factories. A padrone collected the salary of everyone under him, or else a prior fee for placement, and kept a portion for himself as his commission. He also performed sundry tasks like writing letters and sending money back home for those unable to do so themselves. Often, and accurately, accused of taking advantage of those who placed their trust in him—the records of abuses committed by the padrones is replete with decrepit rooming houses and vanishing payrolls—the padrone, nonetheless, performed the valuable services of easing the adjustment to the New World and of obtaining a man's initial position for him. In 1897 two-thirds of the Italian workers in New York were controlled by padrones, but as the immigrant numbers increased and the states began to regulate labor agents, the need for these intermediaries lessened. By the beginning of the twentieth century in Chicago and on the eve of World War I in New York, the number of padrones had declined considerably.

Although the new immigrants had little trouble finding jobs—either with or without the assistance of the padrones—the wages paid rarely provided for a family's subsistence. One scholar discovered that in a Pittsburgh steel district, where a family needed $15 a week to survive, two-thirds of the recent immigrants earned only $12.50 a week, while another third took home less than $10. Tales abound of garment workers earning only 8 cents an hour; others made $1.25 for a full week's work. Prior to World War I residents of New York City required a yearly wage of $876 to maintain a minimum standard of living; yet most families earned less. Although the immigrants earned low wages, some did better than others. In 1901 a government commission reported that Armenians, Jews, and Greeks fared better than Poles, Slovaks, southern Italians, and Serbs.

Wages were especially low for immigrant women who found jobs in the garment industries, laundries, or as domestics. Yet these jobs were more desirable than others. Some immigrant girls who arrived alone and without money ended up as prostitutes in the nation's red-light districts. Indignant and moralistic reformers sometimes exaggerated the extent of the "white slave" traffic, but prostitution certainly grew in the late nineteenth and early twentieth centuries. One muckraking journalist described the plight of the poor immigrant young women in New York City:

> Just north of Houston Street are the long streets of signs where the Polish and Slovak servant-girls sit in stiff rows in the dingy employment agencies, waiting to be picked up as domestic servants. The

odds against these unfortunate, bland-faced farm girls are greater than those against the Galician Jews. They arrive here more like tagged baggage than human beings, are crowded in barracks of boarding-houses, eight and ten in a room at night, and in the morning the runner for the employment agency takes them with all their belongings in a cheap valise, to sit and wait again for mistresses. . . . Just below this section of Poles and Slavs lies the great body of the Jews. . . . These girls are so easily secured that in many cases the men who obtain control of them do not even speak their language.

With life so desolate union organization made firm headway. Garment workers in New York and Chicago went out on strike in 1910 and after long struggles finally won the right to collective bargaining. In an industry run by tyrannical foremen and profit-hungry owners unions like the Amalgamated Clothing Workers and the International Ladies' Garment Workers' Union (ILGWU) pioneered the efforts to establish safety and sanitary codes and to obtain shorter hours and higher wages. The people in the garment trades—owners, workers and union organizers—were predominantly Jewish (and secondarily Italian), and this was the case well into the twentieth century. In 1924 Jews constituted 64 percent of the ILGWU members, and, as late as the 1940s, they made up 75 percent of the members of Dressmakers Local Number 22 in New York City. As the decades passed, however, Jews became concentrated in the upper echelons of management in both factories and unions and were replaced in the rank and file by blacks and Puerto Ricans.

The beginnings of union organization and the continuous replenishment by newer immigrants at the lowest job levels provided the minorities with the opportunities to upgrade their positions and to move away from the slums. It is remarkable, in retrospect, to contemplate how people survived and continued to work and hope for better lives when they were mired in such depressed conditions. Whole neighborhoods were filthy, foul smelling, and overcrowded. In cities like Boston, New York, and Chicago houses adjoined stables, and offal, debris, and horse manure littered the streets. Piles of garbage in front of buildings or in narrow passageways among houses gave rise to stomach-turning odors and a large rat population. The population density was astronomical, some sections of Chicago, for example, having three times as many inhabitants as the most crowded portions of Tokyo and Calcutta. In 1901 a Polish neighborhood in the Windy City averaged 340 people per acre, and a three-block area housed 7,306 children! In the late nineteenth and the early twentieth centuries the Italian sections in New York, Philadelphia, and Chicago seemed little better. One survey taker found that 1,231 Italians were living in 120 rooms in New York, while another reporter could not find a single bathtub in a three-block area of tenements. In Chicago a two- or three-room apartment might house an Italian family of parents, grandparents, several children, boarders, and cousins. A 1910 survey indicated that many of Philadelphia's Italian families had to cook, eat, and sleep in the same room, while most shared outhouses and a water hydrant—the only plumbing facility available—with four or five other families. In addition, many Italians kept chickens in their bedrooms and goats in their cellars. A Jewish girl in a New York tenement described her dwelling as "a place so dark it seemed as if there weren't no sky." In 1901 New York passed a tenement-house law that required all new buildings to have windows 12 feet away from the opposite building, toilets and running water in each apartment, and solid staircases within each structure. But it took many years before a majority of the newcomers occupied such houses.

Although the members of various minority groups shared similar laboring and housing conditions, it would be a mistake to suggest that they also had common values. All, of course, desired decent homes, well-paying jobs, and the opportunity to maintain their own life styles free of strife. But each of the ethnic groups differed in cultural ethos and the ways in which each chose to obtain its goals. Their attitudes toward family, education, religion, success, philanthropy, and community affairs differed considerably from each other. Moreover, the values that the varying groups possessed frequently collided with the dominant strain in this country, a factor that sometimes created new problems for them in the United States.

The non-British minority groups spoke a foreign language when they arrived in America, and this placed an immediate stigma upon them. For their own emotional security they chose to live, like the old immigrants, in neighborhoods inhabited by their compatriots and, as a result, had even less reason to learn English quickly. Immigrant women felt particularly isolated because they rarely left

the insulated community. Even the men were cut off from inter-
action with other groups. This was especially true when they worked
with their compatriots in similar occupations, a situation that further
retarded the assimilating process. As one Italian put it, "When I
arrived in New York I went to live with my *paesani* [countrymen].
I did not see any reason for learning English. I did not need it for
everywhere I lived, or worked or fooled around, there were only
Italians." Habits of dress, food preparation, and religious practices
were also retained by the immigrants. But the young children, educated in the United States, could not accept or feel completely at
home with all of their parents' values. Children of immigrants did
not usually sever all of the Old World ties, nor did most have any
desire to do so, but they did try to harmonize as much of their
parents' culture as they could with the demands of American society.
Inevitably, such harmonization created intergenerational conflicts
and strains. Moreover, the demands of one generation were sometimes in almost total variance with the values of the other.

Italians, for example, placed little importance on *individual*
success or accomplishment. A person was supposed to enhance the
family's fortune or honor, not his own. Only members of the family
and their close blood relations were considered important and could
be trusted. All others outside the family were strangers to whom
one had no responsibilities. Family honor had to be guarded carefully and defended to the death, if necessary, but society's laws were
of little moment. "Individual initiative was virtually unknown," one
scholar tells us, and "all actions had to receive the sanctions of tradition and custom." Most of the Italian immigrants seemed to follow
the advice contained in a southern Italian proverb: "Do not make
your child better than you are."

The Italian *contadini* (peasants), who had a history of oppression, linked education with class, status, and nobility. It was regarded as something that peasants—and women—could not aspire
to. Education might be financed with surplus wealth, but most
immigrant families could barely sustain themselves on what they
earned. The *contadini* also had other reasons for being wary of
the schoolhouse. In Italy, historian Rudolph Vecoli tells us, "educated persons were regarded with mistrust; in the old country, the
priest and professor had been among the exploiters. Immigrant
parents prized education solely for its utilitarian value; reading in

itself was thought to be an idle, and perhaps injurious, pastime."
The southern Italian immigrants, therefore, did not encourage their
children to excel in reading. As soon as the law allowed their offspring were pulled out of school and sent to work. Material, not
cultural, advancement was what counted—the family as a whole
mattered, not the individual child.

Some Italians, of course, did not subscribe to these views. The
first American of Italian descent to become a governor and a United
States senator, Rhode Island's John O. Pastore, had a mother who
was impassioned with achieving American middle-class respectability. She made her sons wear fresh shirts every day and admonished
them, "Make yourself liked; make people respect you." New York
City's first Italian-American school principal recalled his father's
urging, "Go to school. Even if it kills you." But these were the exceptions. Most immigrant-stock Italians achieved a college education only by rejecting their families' values.

The southern Italian attitude toward religion and the church
also differed considerably from that of most Americans and other
immigrants. Nominally Roman Catholic, the Italians as a whole
did not have the attachment for the faith possessed by the Irish.
Unlike American Protestants, who are not always dutiful in their
attendance at church services but who maintain a respect for the
institution and its members, the Italians—partly out of resentment
of its Irish domination—regarded the Church as "a cold and almost
puritanical organization." Moreover, they looked upon the priests
as they had in Italy, "as lazy, ignorant hangers-on who merely
earned their living off the community." It was not that Italians
lacked religious beliefs but rather that their customs were quite different from those of the dominant Irish Catholics. They were flexi-
ble about doctrine, ignorant of many traditional aspects of Roman
Catholicism, and devoted to the festivals and *festas,* which were
more significant to most of them than any part of formal church
services. The southern Italian immigrant feared "the evil eye" and
its effects, and, as one historian tells us, "through the use of
rituals, symbols, and charms, they sought to ward off evil spirits
and to gain the favor of powerful deities." Inevitably, they were
not avid churchgoers, though the women were more faithful than
the men. An 1884 census of 50,000 Italians in New York City
showed that 48,800 of them "neglected church services." Only as
later generations of Italians became Americanized did they adhere

more closely to the dominant standards of the Roman Catholic Church in the United States.

Another point about the Italians that is less true for other immigrants and minorities was their inability to unite for community action. Southern Italians were devoted to their families and had some loyalty to members of their village or community in Italy, but they lacked an overall ethnic commitment. Italian mutual-benefit societies did exist in the United States, but for the most part each one helped comparatively small numbers of Italians. Regional dialects and lack of widespread written communication, as well as a diversity of thought, actions, and life styles, divided Italians of different provinces and regions and made any kind of group organization an almost impossible task in the United States. Not until 1967, in fact, did the Italian-American Civil Rights League band together to protect and defend those of Italian descent in this country from abusive treatment by other Americans.

On the other hand, the success of the Jews in this very area won the admiration of numerous other groups, particularly the Italians. In 1908 when the New York City police commissioner asserted that many criminals were Jewish, the Jewish community of the city protested immediately. A New York Italian newspaper remarked approvingly: "The Jews are all connected to each other, and, when they believe a patent offense has occurred to their colony, they act as one man."

The pogroms in Russia from 1903 to 1906 provided a focus for organized Jewish efforts to help their brethren in distress and out of this came the American Jewish Committee, an organization composed of and representing the Americanized German Jewish community. The committee pledged itself to protect the civil rights of all Jews throughout the world. In 1913 Jews organized another defense organization, B'nai B'rith's Anti-Defamation League (ADL), four weeks after an Atlanta jury convicted a Jew of murder primarily, as B'nai B'rith and other Jews saw it, because he was a Jew. The ADL, dedicated to combating prejudice in the United States wherever it existed, was the first such general defense organization founded in this country and, over the years, has been quite successful in curbing the effects of prejudicial behavior.

The Jews also differed from the Italians in a number of other ways. They were more religiously observant, and, unlike the Italians, becoming more American for Jews meant a weakening rather than a strengthening of religious ties. The Jewish faith, however, embodies ethical prescriptions that make charity a social obligation, and no matter how loose the formal religious bonds most Jews still regard philanthropic activities as an absolute necessity. Moreover, those who seek honor and prestige within the Jewish community know that they will receive both in direct proportion to their generosity and involvement in humanitarian endeavors. It is not surprising, therefore, that by 1909 there were well over 2,000 Jewish charities in the United States in addition to the fraternal organizations, mutual-benefit associations, cemetery groups, Jewish unions, and Zionist-oriented organizations. Jewish philanthropists in that year spent well over $10 million for charity among their coreligionists; the annual budget for Jewish philanthropy now runs over a billion dollars.

Even the German or Americanized Jews, who at first had no desire to see their East European brethren in the United States, engaged in vast philanthropic endeavors to aid the newcomers. Motivation for such activities resulted partly out of a sense of noblesse oblige and partly because they feared that their East European coreligionists might become a burden to society and thereby intensify existing American anti-Semitism. They established orphanages, educational institutions, homes for delinquents and unwed mothers, hospitals, and recreational facilities. They were instrumental also in developing the Jewish Theological Seminary to train Americanized rabbis and a Yiddish language newspaper in the New York City ghetto to help Jewish immigrants adjust to the folkways and mores of this country.

The East European Jews accepted whatever assistance they could, but in addition they endeavored to provide their own facilities. They too established charitable organizations to help the needy. They also devoted themselves to the quest for culture. Between 1885 and 1915 they started over 150 Yiddish language newspapers, journals, and yearbooks. The best known of those, Abraham Cahan's *Forward,* is still published today. At its height before World War I, it was the ghetto's leading journal and over the years the most widely read Yiddish newspaper in this country. In addition Jews established successful theatre groups, and many of their participants, like Paul Muni, Jacob Adler, and Molly Picon, went on to Broadway and Hollywood. The East European Jews attended concerts and lectures and afterward moved on to the most popular cultural institution on the Lower East Side, the café or coffeehouse, where they would debate endlessly about plays, poets, pianists, politics, and the direction society was taking.

More than anything else, however, the Jews sought knowledge. New York City's Educational Alliance had a regular daily attendance of 500 and a waiting list of a thousand for English classes, which were given at all hours of the day and six evenings a week. The poorest families saw to it that their children attended the public school, and teachers generally praised the youngsters for their industry and deportment. By 1915 Jews comprised 85 percent of the student body at New York's free but renowned City College, one-fifth of those attending New York University and one-sixth of the students at Columbia.

Jews who lived outside of New York City did not have the million-plus members of coreligionists to support a full and rounded community life separate from the dominant groups in society. Accordingly, they generally relinquished Old World customs at a faster pace. It is for this very reason, in fact, that first- and second-generation New York City Jews remained where they landed. Rural areas, small towns, and even some of the bigger cities simply could not provide the cultural and educational opportunities as well as the Jewish sense of community so essential to these East European newcomers.

Other immigrants also sought to maintain their own culture in the United States. For the Magyars in America both social and religious life revolved around the church. The Poles were also devoted to the Roman Catholic Church and supported the institution generously. On the other hand, they thought less highly about education or advancing their children's position in society. One Polish American complained that "immigrant parents often thoughtlessly sacrificed their children's future to the exigencies of their own survival, sending them off to jobs when they should still have been in school or college." But the Japanese, Armenians, and Greeks valued learning highly. The Japanese immigrants, who by law could never become citizens themselves, demanded, nevertheless, that their children excel in the American school. Armenian immigrants surpassed all other incoming groups between 1899 and 1910 with a literacy rate of 76 percent. Once in this country they, along with the Japanese and

Greeks, "devoured" education. A common admonition of an Armenian parent to his child went, "My son, don't be ignorant like me— get an education and be a man."

The Greeks also tried to instill in their children the language and heritage of the old country while at the same time making sure they became accomplished in the United States. They encouraged their offspring to prepare for the professions, especially law and medicine, because they were considered the most prestigious fields in Greece. One scholar tells us that among Greek Americans "education of the young became a byword in community after community," while a Chicago schoolteacher claimed, "I think I have found the Greeks the brightest and quickest to learn." Greek-American children performed their required chores, but when someone asked one man why his 14-year-old son was not out working, the father responded, "My boy will stay in school. He must study at home after school. He must be a good student; he must become a good man."

In the Greek-American community the *kinotitos,* or community council, was the governing body of the people. It provided for the establishment of churches and schools, hired and fired priests and teachers, and exerted a constant influence on Greek affairs. One could almost always gauge the feelings of the group by the actions and statements of the *kinotitos.* For recreation the Greeks flocked to their *kuffenein,* or coffeehouses. These served as community social centers where men smoked, drank, conversed, and played games in what became literally a place of refuge after a hard day of work or an escape from dank and dreary living quarters. No Greek-American community was without its *kuffenein,* and one chronicler reported that in Chicago before World War I "every other door on Bolivar Street was a Greek coffee house."

Many of the ethnic groups that came over to the United States felt an attachment or loyalty to their native countries, but none surpassed the Greeks in their devotion to, or involvement with, the homeland. In the United States Greek Americans divided into factions and argued vigorously the ramifications of politics in Greece. Many Greeks did not expect to remain long in the United States, and their fervent attachment to the mother country continued unabated. Although large numbers of Greeks did stay in the United States, they were slow to take out American citizenship, which to many of them meant a renunciation of their heritage.

Whether slow or quick to renounce their past cultures, those immigrants remaining in America saw their children and grandchildren turn away from their heritage. Once begun, the process of assimilation could not be stopped. For most groups each succeeding generation possessed fewer ties to the old country and was more directly involved with American society. They forgot the language of their grandparents, moved away from the urban ghettos, and gained a strong foothold in the mainstream of American life.

Chapter 4

Ethnic Conflict and Immigration Restriction

Although immigrants contributed to the accelerated pace of American growth and development, native Americans did not always consider their presence an unalloyed blessing. Periodically, different groups of Americans wanted to curtail the immigrant traffic, but the overriding national need for more people and the commitment to the idea of America as a haven for the distressed prevented serious legislative curbs. During the colonial period, the Scotch-Irish and the Germans aroused the ire of some, which led to hostile barbs and selective taxation. While John Adams was President, in 1798, the period of naturalization for foreigners was increased from 5 to 14 years, but the law was repealed a few years later. In the middle of the nineteenth century, as we noted, the Know-Nothings again raised the issue of too many foreigners, but then their party evaporated before being able to mount a lengthy campaign.

In the past 100 years, however, numerous pressure groups have succeeded in getting Congress to reduce the number of immigrants allowed to enter the United States. Congess enacted its first restrictive bill in 1875 when it banned prostitutes and alien convicts from American shores. Seven years later a more comprehensive bill excluded lunatics, idiots, and persons likely to become public charges. In 1885 further legislation eliminated contracted laborers. These measures, though reflecting a growing fear of certain types of people, kept out relatively few of those who sought entry into the United States.

More important, the Chinese Exclusion Act of 1882 constituted the first proscription of an ethnic group. The enactment of this law was the culmination of a vigorous West Coast campaign against the Chinese and it reversed the welcome they had originally received during the gold rush in the late 1840s. When, in 1852, the governor of California was seeking new sources of labor for his growing state, he characterized the Chinese as among "the most worthy of our newly adopted citizens."

The negative picture of the Chinese was inaugurated by American missionaries, merchants, and diplomats who had sent back derogatory pictures of China and the Chinese before they came to America. These images were not widely known at first. They did, however, help prepare public opinion for the growing hostility toward Oriental immigrants that developed as their numbers increased from approximately 40,000 in 1860 to over 100,000 in 1880. Although a few opponents of the Chinese acknowledged that Chinese laborers were virtual slaves in this country, most West Coast workers, whether native or foreign-born, insisted that Chinese laborers depressed their wages and, consequently, provided unfair competition. In the 1860s, when the race to complete the transcontinental railroad was in full swing and jobs were abundant, this charge was ignored. When the job was finished, and especially during the depression of the 1870s, virulent anti-Chinese feelings developed in California. One legislative committee in the state, appointed in 1876 to investigate the Chinese in their midst, concluded that "the Chinese are inferior to any race God ever made. . . . [They] have no souls to save, and if they have, they are not worth saving."

Behind much of the anti-Chinese sentiment was racism, the belief that there were vast cultural and racial differences between whites and Orientals. The Chinese were accused of having low morals, specifically of practicing prostitution and smoking opium, of low health standards, and of corrupt influences and practices. One advocate of restriction told a congressional committee in 1877:

> The burden of our accusation against them is that they come in conflict with our labor interests; they can never assimilate with us; that they are a perpetual, unchanging, and unchangeable alien element

that can never become homogeneous; that their civilization is demoralizing and degrading to our people; that they degrade and dishonor labor; that they can never become citizens.

The strength of the movement to ban the Chinese from America centered in California. Mobs assaulted the Chinese; legislatures burdened them with special head taxes; and city ordinances harrassed their hotels and laundries. The most vigorous opposition came from Dennis Kearney and the Workingman's party in the 1870s. One manifesto of this group declared, "the Chinaman must leave our shores. We declare that white men and women, and boys, and girls, cannot live as the people of the great republic should and compete with the single Chinese coolie in the labor market. . . . To an American, death is preferable to life on a par with the Chinaman."

In response to the intense pressure from people on the West Coast, Congress passed the Chinese Exclusion Act of 1882. Loopholes in the law allowed for some immigration, however, and these sparked further agitation and violence in the West. In 1885 a Tacoma mob drove out its Chinese residents and burned their homes, and incidents of violence occurred elsewhere in the West. More Chinese were harassed in Arizona in 1886 than in any other year, and that same year citizens in Tacoma, Washington, burned the community's Chinatown. While awaiting further congressional action California passed its most far-reaching anti-Chinese law. This measure barred all Chinese except governmental officials from entering the state and required those already there to register with state officials. In 1892 additional congressional legislation virtually ended Chinese immigration and restricted the civil rights of those still in this country.

Following these restrictions, overt violence against the Chinese ceased, and agitation for tighter laws and controls gradually subsided. Yet the prejudice against the Chinese remained. Discrimination in jobs and housing was common after 1890, and derogatory images of Chinese Americans appeared in the media. Newspapers played up stories of prostitution, gambling, and opium dens in Chinatowns. "Chinks" and "John Chinaman" were sobriquets frequently used to describe Chinese Americans. The prejudices and discrimination lasted well into the twentieth century. State laws against interracial marriages, for example, were part of the legacy of racial prejudice, and Chinese aliens were not eligible for citizenship until after 1952.

In part Americans transferred their prejudice against the Chinese to the Japanese after the latter began arriving in California and Hawaii in the 1890s. As in the case of anti-Chinese hostility and agitation, the focus of activity was California, where most of the continental Japanese lived. Arguments similar to those used against the Chinese were employed to assail Japanese immigrants. "The Japs must go," shouted one demagogue, while the United States Industrial Commission reported in 1901 that the Japanese were "far less desirable" than the Chinese. "They have most of the vices of the Chinese, with none of the virtues. They underbid the Chinese in everything, and are as a class tricky, unreliable and dishonest."

And yet the racism directed against the Japanese was not the same as the anti-Chinese feeling. Whereas the Chinese were considered coolies who depressed American wages, at times the Japanese were considered too successful, especially in Californian agriculture, in which they became efficient workers and growers. Unlike China, Japan was proving herself to be a world power at the beginning of the twentieth century. Instead of showing contempt for Japan, many racists became alarmed by her growing power. The fear was expressed in the "yellow peril" scare just after 1900. The yellow peril was a visionary invasion of the United States by a horde of millions of Asians. Congressman Richmond Pearson Hobson of Alabama insisted that the yellow peril was already here, and he further warned of war: "The Japanese are the most secretive people in the world" and are "rushing forward with feverish haste stupendous preparations for war. . . . The war is to be with America." The Hearst press in California insisted that "everyone of these immigrants . . . is a Japanese spy."

Growing fear of and antagonism toward Japanese immigrants reached a crisis after the turn of the century. Led by labor groups, delegates gathered in San Francisco in 1905 to organize the Asiatic Exclusion League. A year later, the San Francisco Board of Education ordered the segregation of all Oriental pupils. Of the city's 25,000 schoolchildren only 93 were Japanese, but the public was outraged at reports that older Japanese boys were sitting next to little white girls in classes. The Japanese government protested the order, and Theodore Roosevelt's administration found itself confronted with a full-fledged diplomatic crisis. Federal pressure on the San Francisco school board led to the rescinding of the new policy. In return the Japanese, in the Gentlemen's Agreement of 1907, promised to restrict exit visas for laborers who wanted to go to the United States. The agreement, though it short-circuited a confrontation, did not prevent those Japanese already here from pursuing the American dream. Reputedly hard workers and shrewd businessmen, they amassed a great deal of property before the California legislature, in 1913, prohibited aliens ineligible for citizenship from acquiring land. The act, based on a provision of the naturalization laws limiting citizenship to incoming whites and descendants of Africans, failed in its purpose because the Japanese continued acquiring property in the names of their American-born children or under legal corporate guises.

Californians may have been particularly concerned with Oriental minorities, but the most widespread American hostility was directed at Roman Catholics. The growing Catholic immigrant population after 1880 once more stirred up Protestant bigotry. Even more than before the Civil War, the Roman Catholic Church appeared aggressive and powerful as Irish Catholics succeeded in politics and Catholic leaders spoke without restraint in public.

School issues in particular kindled ethnic tensions. Catholics found the Protestant orientation of American public schools offensive and developed their own parochial schools. Although the Church encouraged all Catholics to send their children to these schools, only a minority of Catholics—mostly of Irish background—chose, or could afford, to do so. This led in turn to Catholic demands for state aid for parochial schools, a proposal that further enraged Protestants. Local elections often centered on the school issue, as did the 1880 elections in New York City, for example. The Democrats had nominated William R. Grace, a Roman Catholic, for the mayoralty, and this incensed a number of the city's Protestants. *The New York Times* stated the prevalent anxieties clearly:

> If the Irish Catholics should happen, for instance, to control the Mayoralty, the Controllership, and the Board of Aldermen, they would very soon be able to reconstitute the Board of Education, to place Catholic Trustees over certain schools, to put in Catholic teachers, to introduce Catholic textbooks, to convey public funds to Church schools under some guise which would elude the law, and, in fact, to Romanize our whole system of public education.

In the end Grace won the election, and the fears expressed by *The New York Times* proved groundless. But the anxieties remained.

Boston, with its large Irish population, was also a hotbed of dispute. In 1889 a public high school teacher defined indulgences in a manner that was considered offensive by a Catholic pupil. The Church protested and the Boston School Committee reprimanded the teacher, transferred him from history to English (a "safer" subject), and dropped a disputed text. Aroused Protestants organized and in the next election won control of the school committee.

At the national level the issue over religion and the schools intruded and divided political parties. In 1875 James G. Blaine, the House Republican leader, proposed a constitutional amendment to ban governmental property or financial aid for the use of any school or other institution under the control of any religious sect. Although the amendment never passed, the issue prompted considerable debate.

At bottom much of the conflict centered on the belief held by many Protestants that Catholicism was a menace to American values and institutions. This view was not as strong as it had been before the Civil War. Nevertheless, many Protestants believed that a large proportion of American Catholics were under the thumb of Rome and were unwilling to accept American values. Some champions of militant Protestantism, in fact, insisted that Catholics had divided loyalties and should be denied the ballot until they took an oath of allegiance renouncing the supremacy of the Pope. A prominent Protestant clergyman, Josiah Strong, expressed much of this anxiety in his popular *Our Country: Its Possible Future and Its Present Crisis* (1885), in which he argued that Catholics gave their foremost allegiance to the Church, not to the United States of America. Protestants like Strong were also agitated because of the Roman Catholic Church's opposition or indifference to the temperance crusade.

The largest anti-Catholic organization to appear in the late nineteenth century was the American Protective Association (A.P.A.). Founded in 1887 in Clinton, Iowa, by Henry Bowers, the A.P.A. had a large following until the mid-1890s; at its peak it claimed 2.5 million members. Appealing mainly to working-class Protestants in the Rocky Mountain States and the Far West, the A.P.A. pledged its members to support the public schools, immigration restriction, and tougher naturalization laws.

To fight the so-called Roman menace the members of the A.P.A. organized boycotts of Catholic merchants, refused to go on strike with Catholic trade unionists, and vowed never to vote for a Roman Catholic for public office. The growing political power of Catholics was especially alarming to the organization, which claimed that "although only one-eighth of the population of the United States was Catholic . . . one-half of all the public officeholders were Catholics . . ., Catholics were favored in the Civil Service examinations, and that all civil servants were forced to contribute to Catholic charities."

Hysteria peaked in 1893 when many believed a rumor that the Pope had written a letter ordering Catholics to exterminate all heretics in the United States. Some Protestants armed themselves, and the mayor of Toledo called out the National Guard to halt the coming slaughter. The outbreak, of course, did not occur, and the rumor soon proved to be groundless and fraudulent, but members of the A.P.A. quickly found other examples of Catholicism to fight.

The association never formed a political party, but it did enter politics. It supported candidates, usually Republicans, who were against the Catholic Church and lobbied for particular pieces of legislation. The association backed state compulsory school-attendance laws and, at the national level, became embroiled in a dispute over Indian schools. Under federal policy established during the Grant administration, contracts were granted to church groups to operate Indian schools. Thus federal funds were going to parochial schools, a policy that horrified the A.P.A. The association threw its support behind efforts to eliminate the contract system and substitute public schools for the church-supported ones.

In spite of the widespread hostility to Catholicism among non-Catholics, the appeal of the association was limited. The movement crested in the 1890s and then fell apart. Other issues were more important to American voters in the 1890s, and the A.P.A. found itself plagued by internal disputes. The Republicans used the A.P.A., but they discovered that it was not important politically. Anti-Catholicism took other forms after 1895.

In addition the religious prejudice directed at Catholics, as we have noted, hostility toward Jews also grew in the late nineteenth century. Anti-Semitism was aggravated by the economic depressions that plagued Americans, on and off, from 1873 through 1896. The German Jews, who arrived in the United States in the middle of the nineteenth century, prospered despite the existing prejudices because there were few, if any, economic barriers to those who were enterprising. Their prosperity in the face of widespread unemployment and despair reinforced the old Shylock image of a cunning and avaricious Jew demanding his pound of flesh. One southern patrician noted, for example, "it is quite the fashion to caricature the Jew as exacting his interest down to the last drachma." He then pointed out, perhaps half in envy and half in respect, that in the hardest of times the Jew "has money to lend if not to burn and before he is ready to execute his will he owns the grocery store, the meat-market, the grog-shop, the planing-mill, the newspaper, the hotel and the bank." The extremist fringe in the free-silver movement saw the Jew as the arch enemy foisting an international gold standard on beleaguered American farmers fighting for silver, "the people's money."

The presence of East European Jews, who started coming to the United States in the 1870s, aggravated existing anti-Semitic feelings; and as we have already noted, all Jews faced growing social and economic discrimination. As Jewish immigration from eastern Europe increased, this anti-Semitism helped to kindle the movement for immigration restriction. In 1906 a member of President Theodore Roosevelt's immigration commission told an investigator that the "movement toward restriction in all of its phases is directed against Jewish immigration. . . ."

Alongside religious antagonisms economic conflicts also confronted the immigrants. Many workingmen opposed immigrants because they claimed the newcomers depressed wages and were potential strikebreakers. The Knights of Labor called for a ban on contract labor, as did a number of labor leaders. Organized labor, with a high proportion of foreign-born workers, was reluctant to support general immigration restriction, but labor leaders were becoming more critical of immigration in the 1880s and in the economically depressed 1890s. In 1897 the American Federation of Labor (AFL), America's largest labor union, finally supported a literacy test as a means of limiting immigration.

Although employers needed workers for the nation's growing industries, at times they were uneasy about immigration. Labor disturbances, fairly common occurrences in the late nineteenth century, were frequently blamed unfairly on foreign agitators. In 1886 policemen broke up a peaceful protest meeting in Chicago. Before the crowd could be dispersed, however, a bomb exploded killing seven policemen. Although no one knew who threw the explosive, the press placed the blame upon foreigners. One newspaper declared that "the enemy forces are not American [but] rag-tag and bob-tail cutthroats of Beelzebub from the Rhine, the Danube, the Vistula, and the Elbe," while another said the German anarchists accused of the crime were "long-haired, wild-eyed, bad-smelling, atheistic, reckless foreign wretches, who never did an honest hour's work in their lives."

Especially important in the growing development of nativism was the fact that Americans became aware of the increased immigration from southern and eastern Europe. As previously noted, Americans considered these new immigrants to be of a different culture, undesirable, unassimilable, and hostile or indifferent to American values. Stereotyped images of Slavs, Jews, and especially Italians appeared. To the nativist, Italians suggested an image of crime and violence. As a Baltimore newspaper put it, "The disposition to assassinate in revenge for a fancied wrong is a marked trait in the character of this impulsive and inexorable race." Anti-Italian sentiment led to the lynching of 11 Italians in New Orleans in 1891. After the murder of a police superintendent, suspicion fell upon the local Sicilian community and several Italians were indicted. City officials called for stern action, but the jury refused to convict. An angry mob then took matters into its own hands and lynched the accused men.

Late nineteenth-century Americans were increasingly receptive to pseudoracial thinking that divided Europeans into different races. In other words, Slavs, Jews, and Italians constituted races rather than nationalities or ethnic groups. According to this kind of thinking, differences were emphasized and one "race" was deemed to be superior to another. This point of view became more important in the early twentieth century. Not surprisingly, the racists found the old immigrants superior and more desirable than the new, or as one alarmed nativist said, "It is only in recent years that new, more ignorant and therefore more dangerous elements have entered into the problem of immigration. . . . The Irish and German tides were ebbing, while those of Southern and Eastern Europe were both increasing and threatening. None but an optimist of the purest water can view it without concern."

Just as religious prejudice, economic rivalry, and intellectual racism generated opposition to immigration, so did politics. Urban reformers noted with apprehension the rise of the Irish and then other ethnic minorities in urban politics. Reformers, usually those of old stock, believed that political machines built on immigrant votes were corrupt and inefficient, the protectors of prostitution, graft, and saloons. Prostitution was considered a virtual immigrant monopoly. A reform group in the 1890s declared, "unless we make energetic and successful war upon the red light districts . . . we shall have Oriental brothel slavery thrust upon us. . . . Jew traders, too, will people our 'levees' with Polish Jewesses and any others who will make money for them. Shall we defend our American civilization, or lower our flag to the most despicable foreigners—French, Irish, Italians, Jews, and Mongolians?" Not until the power of the immigrant-supported machine was broken, they argued, could American cities be reformed.

Not all reformers regarded the immigrant as the cause of corruption; many attributed political corruption to business influence, and they noted that immigrants supported machines because the machine helped them. Clean up the immigrants' environment, they said, and the machine would lose its following. Yet graft and the social ills of American cities, combined with the concentration of immigrants in the urban ghettos, too often led native Americans to blame political chicanery on immigrants.

Not all ethnic conflict was native versus immigrant. Many of the newcomers distrusted and disliked one another. Irishman Dennis Kearney, leader of the California Workingmen's party, led the assault on the Chinese, and English-born Samuel Gompers of the AFL favored immigration restriction. Within the ranks of labor some foreign-born unionists did not want members of ethnic groups other than their own in their unions. Foreign-born Protestants, as within the A.P.A., did not trust Catholic immigrants. Within the Catholic Church itself Germans, French Canadians, Italians, and Poles resented Irish domination. As one Polish journal remarked in 1900, "Is it that the Irish want to dominate the Catholic world? Can't Polish Catholics have as much freedom as the other nationalities? Isn't the United States a land of Freedom? It is, but that is no reason that the Irish should have more preference than any other nationality." Europeans came to America with fears and prejudices about others, and these did not disappear immediately. When German votes killed a proposal to teach Bohemian in a Chicago school, Bohemians retorted, "Finally, since impudence, selfishness, obstinacy and insolence is [sic] excessively rooted in the minds of all Germans, almost without exception, how then could we expect, even in this land of freedom to receive any support from them."

The xenophobia of the 1880s and 1890s pointed inevitably in one direction: immigration restriction. Although the Chinese were banned in 1882 and the first general federal immigration law of that year had excluded certain classes of immigrants, these laws did not greatly affect the flow of immigration traffic. Bigots called for drastic limitations. The time had come, they insisted, to decide whether the nation was "to be peopled by British, German and Scandinavian stock, historically free, energetic, progressive, or by Slav, Latin and Asiatic races, historically down-trodden, atavistic, and stagnant." The most popular scheme for stemming the tide was the literacy test. Led by the Immigration Restriction League, founded in Boston in 1894 by Boston blue bloods, agitation for federal action grew. The literacy test, which required immigrants over 16 to be literate in some language, made no distinctions among nationalities or races, but the intent of the proposal was clear. Since proportionately more northern and western Europeans than southern and eastern Europeans were literate, the literacy requirement would have barred the latter groups of immigrants from the United States.

The literacy test, supported by the Republican party, finally did pass in 1896, only to be vetoed by President Grover Cleveland, who insisted that America should remain an asylum for the oppressed of Europe. The President also rejected the inference that the new immigrants were less desirable than the old: "It is said," he declared, "that the quality of recent immigration is undesirable. The time is quite within recent memory when the same thing was said of immigrants who, with their descendants, are now numbered among our best citizens." The literacy test's proponents attempted to muster the votes to override the veto, but they failed. And then the tide of nativism ebbed somewhat after 1896 as prosperity returned.

But it quickly reappeared and by 1901 President Theodore Roosevelt was speaking in a vein quite different from that used by Cleveland only a few years earlier. Stirred by the recent assassination of President William McKinley by an anarchist, Roosevelt called for a comprehensive immigration act to keep out "not only all persons who are known to be believers in anarchistic principles or members of anarchistic societies, but also all persons who are of a low moral tendency or of unsavory reputation" and "all persons . . . who are below a certain standard of economic fitness to enter our industrial field as competitors with American labor." The President also wanted a careful educational test to ascertain the capacity to "appreciate American institutions and act sanely as American citizens." Roosevelt insisted that his proposals would decrease the "sum of ignorance" in America and "stop the influx of cheap labor, and the resulting competition which gives rise to so much of the bitterness in American industrial life, and it would dry up the springs of the pestilential social conditions in our great cities, where anarchist organizations have their greatest possibility of growth." Congress responded in part to the President's request by excluding anarchists in 1903 and "imbeciles, feeble-minded [persons] and persons with physical or mental defects which might affect their ability to earn a living" four years later.

In 1907 Congress also appointed a joint Senate-House commission to investigate the entire immigration problem. The new commission, known by the name of its chairman, Senator William Paul Dillingham of Vermont, issued a 42-volume report in 1911. Its main assumption was that the newer immigrants from southern and eastern Europe were more ignorant, more unskilled, more prone to crime, and more willing to accept a lower standard of living than the older immigrants from northern and western Europe. The newcomers, the commission announced, were "content to accept wages and conditions which the native American and immigrants of the older class had come to regard as unsatisfactory." Although the Dillingham Commission did not favor a direct ban on the new immigration (it preferred a literacy test instead), it did suggest that restrictive legislation could be based upon a percentage of each nationality group already in the United States. This alternative was ignored at the time but would be revived a decade later.

Congress responded to the Dillingham report with the passage of another literacy bill in 1913, but once again a President would not sanction it. William Howard Taft, heeding protests from friends favoring liberal immigration policies, acknowledged an "abiding faith" in American institutions to exert a positive influence upon newcomers "no matter how lacking in education they may be. . . . The second generation of a sturdy but uneducated peasantry," he continued, "brought to this country and raised in an atmosphere of thrift and hard work, and forced by their parents into school and to obtain an instrument for self-elevation, has always contributed to the strength of our people, and will continue to do so." The outbreak of World War I and American entry into the war in 1917 broke the dam holding back the tide of nativism. Congress again passed a literacy bill, and when President Woodrow Wilson for a second time refused to approve it, Congress overrode his veto.

In the heated atmosphere of wartime, patriots insisted upon 100 percent Americanism. Radical opponents of the war and German Americans who were suspected of having pro-German sentiments or of being secret agents of the Kaiser became targets of unrestrained hysteria. Theodore Roosevelt led the attack on German Americans and insisted that "the men of German blood who have tried to be both German and American are not Americans at all, but traitors to America and tools and servants of Germany against America." Superpatriots attacked German Americans, their organizations, and their press. Libraries removed German books from their shelves, and several states, among them Delaware, Iowa, and Montana, prohibited public schools from teaching German. Sauerkraut became "liberty cabbage," orchestras refused to perform German music, and towns, business firms, and people hastily anglicized their German-sounding names. Pittsburgh, Pennsylvania, for example, added an *h* to its spelling so as to look more Scottish than German. Angry mobs sometimes smashed German stores and occasionally burned German books. That most German Americans were loyal to the nation and supported the war did not seem to matter.

Although they were not as suspect as German Americans, some Irish Americans also came under attack. Many people of Irish ancestry were unenthusiastic about fighting a war in alliance with Great Britain, who was regarded as the traditional enemy and oppressor of Ireland. A few Irish Americans who were critical of the Wilson administration found themselves in difficulty with the law.

The xenophobia unleashed by the war reached new heights in the 1920s. Although German and Irish Americans now found more acceptance, immigrants and their children were generally suspect. The nation assumed an isolationist mood; old-stock Americans rejected Europe and her peoples and insisted on conformity and loyalty to the nation. The Russian Revolution, a by-product of the war, added to the fears of things foreign. Americans believed that radical ideology, which was long suspect and considered a foreign import, had to be stamped out or suppressed. Radical groups found themselves hounded and physically assaulted, and Attorney General

A. Mitchell Palmer's Justice Department rounded up aliens in spectacular raids and deported them during the Red Scare of 1919. Patriotic groups bombarded Congress with petitions proclaiming the time had arrived "when Americans should assert themselves and drive from these shores all disloyal aliens."

While conservative and patriotic groups feared radical agitators flooding America with their Bolshevik ideas, labor leaders feared cheap labor. The 1920s were lean years for organized labor, as the unions lost over 1 million members. In 1918 the AFL, anxious about the problems of industrial reconversion after the war, called for a two-year halt in immigration. Some labor union leaders not only used the old cheap-foreign-labor argument, but they also warned about the social dangers of immigration. As was noted before, the English-born Gompers, president of the AFL, defended restriction: "America has not yet become a nation." He noted that it was "honeycombed with 'foreign groups' living a foreign life," and this would continue if the nation's door remained open to all comers.

The 1920s have been described as a tribal era during which ethnocentrism and xenophobia ran wild. No development better illustrates this situation than the activities of the Ku Klux Klan, the largest nativist organization of the 1920s, which claimed over 4 million members at its height. Founded in Georgia in 1915, the Klan had a spectacular growth rate in the early 1920s and for a brief period exerted considerable political clout in several states including Indiana, Alabama, Texas, and Florida. Klansmen thundered at liberal Protestantism and modern ideas and demanded prohibition enforcement and compulsory Bible reading in the public schools. But the focus of their credo was anti-black, anti-Semitic, anti-Catholic, and anti-immigrant. Hiram W. Evens, the Klan's Imperial Wizard, believed that the "old-stock Americans," the "Nordic race" of peoples, had "given the world almost the whole of modern civilization." And he insisted that the aliens from eastern and southern Europe should be kept out of the United States.

The Klan's response to immigration and minorities was merely an extreme version of what many old-stock white Protestants believed. Prohibitionists, for example, insisted there was a sinister connection between liquor, the city, and the immigrant. One liberal clergyman claimed that "National Prohibition is the highest mark of distinctively American morality and citizenship" and warned, "There is already too much congestion of immigrants in the great cities. . . .

If we are to have an American civilization we must assimilate the stream of newcomers. If we do not assimilate them they will adulterate us with an admixture of old-world morals. A straw in the wind is afforded by the recent referendum in Massachusetts on the liquor issue. The entire state went overwhelmingly dry except the large immigrant filled cities, and they went so overwhelmingly wet as to give the state as a whole a wet majority."

From Michigan, Henry Ford's *Dearborn Independent* published anti-Semitic diatribes not dissimilar to those of the Klan. Included in the *Dearborn Independent*'s vitriolic writings were the *Protocols of the Elders of Zion*. This fake document, concocted by the Russian secret police at the turn of the century, claimed there was a Jewish plot to establish a world dictatorship. During the decade, anti-Semitism even reached the hallowed gates of Harvard University when the university's administration established a Jewish quota, thereby prompting one Jew to dub the school an "intellectual Ku Klux Klan."

Intellectual racism peaked in the early 1920s. The eugenics movement in America after 1900 had warned of the dangerous effects of bad heredity. Eugenicists said that it was poor hereditary factors rather than environmental factors that produced unalterable human inequalities. Some anthropologists and other social scientists supported racist thinking. Racist popularizers, such as Madison Grant, enjoyed a vogue in the 1920s. Grant's *The Passing of the Great Race,* first published in 1916, and Lothrop Stoddard's *The Rising Tide of Color* preached a racism that could easily be applied to immigration restriction. Grant declared:

> These new immigrants were no longer exclusively members of the Nordic race as were the earlier ones who came of their own impulse to improve their social conditions. The transportation lines advertised America as a land flowing with milk and honey, and the European governments took the opportunity to unload upon careless, wealthy, and hospitable America the sweepings of their jails and asylums. The result was that the new immigration ... contained a large and increasing number of the weak, the broken, and the mentally crippled of all races drawn from the lowest stratum of the Mediterranean basin and the Balkans, together with hordes of the wretched, submerged populations of the Polish Ghettos.

A follower of Grant argued that continued immigration would inevitably produce "a hybrid race of people as worthless and futile as the good-for-nothing mongrels of Central America and Southeastern Europe," while a psychologist, flushed with uncritical use of results of IQ tests, proclaimed that the "intellectual superiority of our Nordic group over the Alpine, Mediterranean and Negro groups has been demonstrated."

Given the intense nativism of the 1920s, the issue was not *whether* there would be immigration restriction but *what form* it would take. Aside from the recent immigrants few Americans, regardless of their backgrounds, resisted restriction. Congressmen representing urban areas with heavy concentrations of the foreign-born, however, attacked the proposed laws and their racist assumptions, but they lacked the votes to sustain their views. Over 800,000 newcomers arrived in 1921, and foes of immigration had visions of another immigrant invasion after the wartime lull. Stories circulated of between 5 and 20 million Europeans ready to descend upon the United States.

In 1921 Congress finally established the principle of restriction based on nationality and placed a ceiling on immigration from Europe. The 1921 law, for a one-year period, limited the number of entrants of each nationality to 3 percent of the foreign-born of that group in America based on the 1910 census. Under this stopgap measure approximately 358,000 were eligible to come from Europe. Congress extended the law twice before passing the Johnson-Reed Immigration Act of 1924.

The Johnson-Reed bill continued the qualifications enacted in the past, such as the exclusion of anarchists, prostitutes, illiterates, and those likely to become public charges, and it also tightened the quotas established three years earlier. Fully operative in 1929, the act established a total quota of 153,714, excluding the Western Hemisphere (Orientals had already been excluded by the Oriental Exclusion Act of 1924). Under the new system each nation received an immigration allowance equivalent to its proportion of the nation's 1920 population.

A presidential commission, created by the 1924 act, appointed a distinguished panel to determine the national allocation. The experts concluded that of the 94.8 million whites in the 1920 population, 41.3 million were of colonial stock and 53.5 million of postcolonial stock. Over three quarters of the colonial group were of British origin, and of the postcolonial group 65 percent came from northern and western Europe. Thus the quotas heavily favored the English and countries in northern and western Europe, which was precisely what Congress and the President wanted. The Great Britain-Northern Ireland quota was 44 percent of the total, being 65,361. Ireland was granted 17,756; Germany 25,814; and the Scandinavian countries 6,872. By comparison Italy was allotted 5,802; Poland 6,524; and Russia 2,784. Some nation's quotas were so small under this formula that the act permitted them a maximum of 100. Thus countries like Syria, Albania, and Turkey received the lowest allotment. The exclusion of the Western Hemisphere kept the door open for heavy immigration from Mexico, South America, and Canada until Congress finally placed curbs on migrants from the Western Hemisphere in 1965.

The passage of the Johnson-Reed Act marked the end of an era in American history. Orientals had already been excluded, but Europeans, who comprised the vast bulk of millions of immigrants coming to America, had found the nation an open door. The act ended this virtually free-immigration policy, and although the United States would loosen the act's restrictions and eventually replace them with others, the country did not return to free immigration from Europe again.

Chapter 5

Changing Patterns of Immigration

THE immigration restriction acts of the 1920s, combined with the severe depression of the 1930s, produced the effect that restrictionists had been clamoring for: drastically reduced numbers of people coming into the United States. When the final quota system went into effect in 1929, President Herbert Hoover requested that the State Department use its administrative powers for a tight enforcement of the laws. In particular, the likely-to-become-a-public-charge provision of the immigration codes was invoked, for America experienced a deep economic depression during the 1930s and did not want foreign laborers to compete with the growing numbers of unemployed native workers seeking jobs. Actually, few wanted to emigrate to America during the early stages of the depression. Only 23,068 came in 1933; 28,470 in 1934; and 34,956 in 1935. In several years more persons left the nation than arrived; there were simply not enough jobs to go around, and few and inadequate relief benefits were available.

Before the immigration acts and the depression combined to curb the large numbers of newcomers, Filipinos moved into Hawaii and California to fill the labor gap created by the restriction of other Orientals. The commonwealth status of the Philippines to the United States meant that there were no legal barriers preventing movement; the enormous needs of the sugar planters in Hawaii and the farmers in California provided the spur. The majority of those who came to the United States were of the lower classes and conversed in the Ilocano dialect.

Filipinos had been emigrating to Hawaii to work for the sugar and pineapple planters since the Gentlemen's Agreement of 1907 with Japan had reduced Japanese emigration. In the next quarter century the Hawaiian Islands welcomed 125,000 Filipinos. In the 1920s, however, when California growers feared that Congress might impose quotas on Mexicans, they turned to the Filipinos for labor. Filipinos came to the mainland from Hawaii and directly from the Philippine Islands. According to 1920 census figures, there were only 5,603 Filipinos on the mainland, but ten years later they numbered 45,208. Other sources estimate that there may have been more than twice that number. Ninety percent of the Filipinos were single, male, and under 30 years of age. They worked in northern and central California farms and vineyards. Stockton, California, with a concentration of perhaps 4,000 to 8,000 Filipinos, became known at the end of the 1920s as the Manila of California, while other sizable settlements formed in San Francisco, Seattle, and Portland.

The commonwealth status of the Philippines also permitted substantial numbers of Filipinos to be recruited for the United States armed forces, especially the navy. This accounted for the presence of Filipino communities in the San Diego and Los Angeles areas. The majority of these recruits made the military their career and left the service only upon retirement. The armed forces provided them with security and, more important, with the chance to bring their families to the United States. In the navy the Filipinos were usually assigned to mess halls and as personal attendants to high-ranking military personnel.

The depression and American prejudices caused many Filipinos to lose their jobs during the 1930s. A congressional act of 1934, which promised the Philippine Islands their independence ten years later, also established an annual Filipino quota of 50 immigrants. The quota, plus the fact that many Filipinos returned home, cut their numbers in West Coast agriculture; by 1940 90 percent of those who remained in California were found working in such personal domestic service jobs as bellboys, houseboys, cooks, kitchen helpers, and waiters.

As economic conditions improved in the late 1930s, increased numbers of Europeans again began emigrating to America. More important as motivating factors than economics, however, were the triumph of fascism in Germany in 1933 and the coming of war in Europe six years later. As the Germans annexed Austria (1938) and Czechoslovakia (1939) and then crushed Poland (1939) and conquered Norway, Denmark, the Netherlands, Belgium, and France in the spring of 1940, hundreds of thousands fled in terror, and more would have left had they been able to do so.

Many who ran away were opponents of Nazism. University professors, politicians, and church leaders who openly opposed Hitler either escaped Nazi-dominated countries or were hounded from their posts and thrown into prison. Eventually, many of those in opposition who did not flee ended up in concentration camps or were executed.

Though thousands of political and religious dissenters were persecuted by Hitler's regime, the major victims of the Nazis were the Jews. Plagued by numerous harassments, legal and otherwise, Jews sought asylum in other countries. After accepting as many as they thought they could absorb, the nations of the world refused any further modifications in their immigration policies. Until 1939 Hitler permitted almost all Jews who chose to leave to do so; unfortunately, most could not find any nation that would accept them. The horrors perpetrated on the Jews by the Nazis were legion, but, before the mass exterminations in the concentration camps, perhaps the worst single episode occurred on the night of November 9–10, 1938. The government sanctioned a savage assault on German Jews, and throughout the night people were beaten, stores were looted, and homes, hospitals and old-age institutions were burned; at least 20,000 people were rounded up for deportation to concentration camps. The vicious barbarity of these actions evoked world-wide denunciation. President Franklin D. Roosevelt declared, "I myself could scarcely believe that such things could occur in a twentieth-century civilization."

Nevertheless, United States immigration laws remained intact, and the American government made few allowances for the victims of Hitler's terroristic policies. Americans certainly feared economic competition from immigrant workers, for with almost 10 million unemployed in the United States, job prospects for newcomers were dim. The likelihood that additional people in the country would merely become public charges and swell overburdened relief roles was not discounted either. A few Americans also believed that spies and fifth-column agents would enter as refugees if quotas were eased. But especially important in the opposition to relaxing existing quotas was a strong tinge of anti-Semitism in the United States.

President Franklin Roosevelt was aware of American hostility toward Jews, yet he also sympathized with the refugees' plight, as did a number of Americans who urged the nation to assist them. Roosevelt instructed members of the consulate service to grant them "the most humane and favorable treatment under the law," which enabled some refugees to come to America; generally the President was willing to let the State Department handle the situation. Unfortunately, anti-Semitism existed in the United States State Department too, and its influence resulted in a rigid application of the visa policy against Jewish applicants. Typical of this attitude was the Assistant Secretary of State, Breckenridge Long, who had charge of refugee affairs after 1939. In 1941 he recorded approval, in his diary, of another man's opposition to further immigration. "He said," Long wrote, that "the general type of intending immigrant was just the same as the criminal Jews who crowd our police court dockets in New York. . . . I think he is right. . . ."

The State Department position probably reflected the majority viewpoint in the United States. When, in 1939, Senator Robert F. Wagner of New York and Congresswoman Edith Rogers of Massachusetts proposed a measure to allow 20,000 German refugee children between the ages of 6 and 14 years into the United States above the quota limit, patriotic societies like the American Legion and the Daughters of the American Revolution denounced it. In speaking against the legislation a spokeswoman for the Ladies of the Grand Army of the Republic warned that Congress might "decide to admit 20,000 German-Jewish children!" A year later, however, when mercy ships started bringing children from Great Britain to the United States, patriotic organizations voiced no opposition, and congressional mail ran heavily in approval. Over 15,000 American families each volunteered to take one of the British children with "a blond English girl, 6 years old" seemingly the most popular choice.

Anti-Semitism reached its zenith in the United States in the late 1930s. Groups like the Silver Shirts and the German-American Bund thundered against the Jews. Bigots saw the "hidden hand of international Jewry" around every corner, and patriots organized

"Buy Christian" campaigns. The most influential and well-known anti-Semite was the radio priest Father Charles E. Coughlin. Originally a supporter of the New Deal, Coughlin turned against Roosevelt and increasingly used anti-Jewish and anti-communist arguments in his broadcasts and journal, *Social Justice*. This journal reprinted excerpts from the discredited *Protocols of the Elders of Zion* and carried a speech by the German Propaganda Minister Joseph Goebbels. *Social Justice* had an estimated circulation of over 300,000, and millions heard Coughlin's radio voice. In 1940 and 1941 public-opinion polls revealed that from 17 to 20 percent of the nation considered Jews "a menace to America." Another 12 to 15 percent admitted that they would support an anti-Semitic campaign, and still others indicated that they would be sympathetic to such a campaign.

Despite the existent bigotry, though, Jews, as well as others who came to America under the quota system, received hospitable treatment. A host of organizations, like the National Refugee Service, the Hebrew Immigrant Aid Society, and various ad hoc groups, stood ready to assist the newcomers in finding jobs, housing, and friends.

European arrivals in the 1930s included a number of eminent intellectuals and scientists. Albert Einstein was perhaps the best known of the illustrious immigrants, as they have been called, but other Nobel prizewinners also came during the decade. Among the most noted of these were Thomas Mann, the writer; Bruno Walter and Arturo Toscanini, the conductors; Paul Tillich, the theologian; Béla Bartók, the composer; and Enrico Fermi, the physicist. Several of the scientists who came later played key roles in the development of the atomic bomb.

Those who arrived in the 1930s usually adjusted to America more readily than most of the millions who had come before them. The professionals and many refugees were well educated, often knew English, and had contacts and skills that they could utilize in the United States. Fleeing in terror from Europe, they were eager to become American citizens and to participate in American society. One such refugee was Henry Kissinger, who would later serve as President Richard Nixon's chief foreign-policy adviser and in 1973 would become America's first foreign-born Secretary of State.

Not all could adapt as well, however. Béla Bartók, the composer, never felt at home in America and died in relative obscurity
and poverty in New York City in 1945. Some, like Thomas Mann,
returned to Europe after the war. Others who lacked the contacts
of an Einstein or a Toscanini had to take jobs where they could
find them, often beneath their educational level and skills. The fact
that they sometimes left families and friends behind to an unknown
fate also added to their anxieties.

Concern that fifth-column agents would enter America if quotas
were relaxed may have been one factor blocking a change in immigration laws, but fear of sabotage by enemy aliens already here was
even greater during World War II. Consequently, the federal government interned a few Germans and Italians and carefully watched
others during the war. Japanese aliens and American citizens of
Japanese ancestry, however, fared quite differently. Most of them on
the West Coast were incarcerated in relocation centers that some
critics likened to concentration camps.

Certainly, the fear of espionage, heightened by the surprise attack
on Pearl Harbor and rumors of attacks to come on the mainland,
were real factors in prompting the federal government to intern
Japanese Americans. In spite of the fact that no acts of espionage
or sabotage by Japanese Americans were uncovered in either
Hawaii or California, the boards of supervisors of 11 California
counties solemnly declared that "during the attack on Pearl Harbor
... the Japanese were aided and abetted by fifth columnists of the
Japanese." One United States senator insisted:

> ... a Jap born on our soil is a subject of Japan under Japanese
> law; therefore he owes allegiance to Japan.... The Japanese are
> among our worst enemies. They are cowardly and immoral. They
> are different from Americans in every conceivable way, and no
> Japanese ... should have a right to claim American citizenship. A
> Jap is a Jap anywhere you find him, and his taking the oath of
> allegiance to this country would not help, even if he should be per-
> mitted to do so. They do not believe in God and have no respect for
> an oath. They have been plotting for years against the Americans
> and their democracies.

Even when others pointed out that no espionage had been reported,
proponents of internment argued that that merely proved the danger was greater, for the Japanese were tricky, sneaky and under-
handed, plotting for the right moment to subvert America. Ironi-

cally, the very absence of overt sabotage was held against them. It was, said General John DeWitt, "a disturbing and confirming indication that such action would be taken[!]"

Behind the discussions of potential disloyalty lay years of racial antagonism toward the Japanese in America. The Oriental Exclusion Act of 1924 slammed the door shut for Japanese and other Asian immigrants, but it did not end racism. Various California patriotic and nativist groups hated or mistrusted the Japanese in their midst and considered them unassimilable and treacherous. Economic conflicts also influenced attitudes toward the Japanese. Some small businessmen and farmers envied their economic success in California agriculture and business. The war clouds gathering in the Far East during the 1930s also added to the fears of Japan and the Japanese.

The attack on Pearl Harbor rekindled the old fears and prejudices and prompted new outbreaks of anti-Japanese hysteria. Demands arose to remove Japanese Americans from the Pacific Coast, and in February 1942 President Roosevelt issued Executive Order 9066, one of the most infamous presidential orders in American history. Under this action, which was later backed by a congressional law, the army rounded up approximately 110,000 West Coast Japanese, most of whom were native-born American citizens, and placed them in ten camps called relocation centers, scattered throughout the western United States. In Hawaii, where prejudice was less intense and the Japanese played a more important role in the economy, only a few were interned.

The hasty removal meant considerable hardship and suffering. Given only five days' notice of the evacuation, those interned could take only what they could carry; the government sequestered all other belongings. In addition to the financial losses the conditions in the relocation centers were miserable. At first the Japanese were placed in temporary quarters, including a hastily converted race track, which lacked basic amenities. Eventually, the government built ten camps, but they were mostly located in barren desert country, hot in the summer and cold in winter. The surroundings were drab and unattractive, complete with barbed wire, military police, and, in some instances, machine guns. One Nisei intern later wrote of the camp in Poston, Arizona: "I must say this scorching Hell is a place beyond description and beyond tears." Gradually, conditions for the internees improved except for those

persons considered especially disloyal, who were placed at the Tule
Lake, California, camp. In 1944 the United States Supreme Court
upheld the evacuation and detention of the Japanese Americans.

When the government closed the camps in 1945, Japanese Americans were fearful about how they would fare in the United States.
Some of the most bitter renounced their American citizenship and
returned to Japan. The majority, though, elected to return to California despite federal efforts to relocate them elsewhere. Anti-
Japanese groups in California opposed their return. Bumper stick-
ers appeared declaring "No Japs Wanted in California," and a
few incidents occurred, especially in the Central Valley of the
Golden State. Veterans groups urged boycotts of reopened Japanese-American businesses, and a few rocks were thrown and shots
fired into the homes of Japanese Americans. In Oregon an American Legion post removed the names of local Japanese-American
servicemen from the public honor roll, and other American Legion
posts on the West Coast banned Japanese-American servicemen
from membership.

Yet the opposition gradually subsided, and, aided by church and
liberal civic groups, Japanese Americans were able to find homes,
jobs, and increasing acceptance. They were able to reclaim, however, only about a tenth of their $400 million in forfeited holdings.
In 1948 an anti-Japanese proposition on the California ballot to
make the alien laws harsher was defeated by 59 percent of the
voters. Although over 40 percent still favored restrictions against
the Japanese, this was the first time in Californian history that
an anti-Japanese referendum had been defeated. In 1952 the
California Supreme Court declared the 1913 Alien Land Act un-
constitutional, and Congress removed another restriction against
the Japanese the same year. In 1952 the McCarran-Walter Immigration Act lifted the ban on Asian immigration and the exclusion of Asians from citizenship. Japanese Americans still faced
discrimination in the 1950s and 1960s, however, especially in housing and jobs, but the situation had changed drastically from pre–
World War II attitudes and practices. By the 1960s public-
opinion polls revealed that most Americans considered Japanese
Americans desirable citizens, trustworthy people, and loyal to the
United States. Nevertheless, the trauma for those interned has not
been completely overcome. A generation after the camps closed
one Japanese American admitted, "My father still trembles when

he talks about this experience." On Memorial Day, 1974, some Japanese Americans, whose children had difficulty in believing the stories of their parents' hardships, made a pilgrimage to the Tule Lake camp. In Klamath Falls, Oregon, where a few had stopped to pay respects to those who had died at Tule Lake, a woman passing by rolled down her car window and shouted, "You're on the wrong side of the ocean."

Like anti-Japanese sentiment, anti-Semitism declined but did not disappear following the war. Public-opinion polls indicated that fewer Christians believed Jews to be greedy, dishonest, or unscrupulous; and overt anti-Semitism, so commonly expressed by journals and right-wing groups in the 1930s, became less frequent and less respectable. Accompanying the drop in prejudicial attitudes towards Jews was the decline of social and economic discrimination. Universities and professional schools eliminated Jewish quotas, and business firms previously averse to hiring Jews modified their policies. Changes in major corporations and law firms came slowly. A symbolic landmark was established in December 1973, when E. I. DuPont, the world's largest chemical company, chose Irving S. Shapiro, the son of East European Jewish immigrants, as its president and chief executive officer.

Another persistent theme in American history, anti-Catholicism, also subsided after World War II. Conflicts between Protestants and Catholics continued over aid to parochial schools, a proposed American ambassador to the Vatican, the relations of church and state, publicly sponsored birth-control clinics, and abortion. But the deep emotional strife of the past declined sharply. The ecumenical movement of the postwar society brought Protestants, Catholics, and Jews together in new areas of cooperation. In this same spirit Pope Paul VI visited the United States in 1965, conducted a prayer service before 70,000 people in New York's Yankee Stadium, and received a warm welcome.

The decline of prejudice can be explained by several factors. The fear of divided loyalties that was so potent in World War I and, to a lesser extent, in World War II did not materialize during the cold war. Prejudice is also strongly correlated with levels of income, religious intensity, and education. As incomes and education increased and as religion became less of a commitment and more of a social identification, tolerance grew. Education did not guarantee the end of prejudice, as upper-class prejudice certainly remained, but there is no doubt that the rising levels of education served to dampen the fires of bigotry. A highly educated public seemed more willing to accept ethnic differences. At the same time, minority members absorbed the dominant values of society as they went through the schools and state colleges and universities. Finally, as a result of the immigration laws of the 1920s, the nation had achieved a general balance of ethnic groups. Old-stock Americans no longer feared being overrun by hordes of aliens who might undermine their traditions and destroy their institutions. The foreign-born percentage of the population steadily declined from about one-seventh in the 1920s to less than one-twentieth by the 1970s. America was becoming a more homogenized nation as the grandchildren of European immigrants came to be indistinguishable from one another or, indeed, from those whose ancestry predates the American Revolution.

The abatement of ethnic conflict and the general prosperity of post–World War II America created a climate suitable for the modification of the severe immigration acts. The war and re-shuffling of national boundaries resulted in enormous damage to homes, factories, cities, and towns throughout Europe and made many persons homeless and unable or unwilling to return to their native lands. To meet this situation President Harry S. Truman inaugurated a shift in immigration policy when he issued a directive on December 22, 1945, admitting 40,000 refugees or displaced persons. Congress, desirous of reuniting families of servicemen, passed the War Brides Act of 1946, which eventually enabled 120,000 wives, grooms, and alien children of members of the armed forces to emigrate to the United States. Assisting masses of refugees proved more difficult. Truman's 1945 directive was an emergency step, and it took considerable political pressure before the Congress also responded. Finally, in 1948, the Displaced Persons Act won approval after it had been all but mutilated by opponents of a liberal immigration policy. President Truman signed the bill reluctantly and denounced its provisions, which, he said, discriminated "in callous fashion against displaced persons of the Jewish faith." In 1950, after most of the Jewish refugees had gone to Israel, Congress amended the 1948 act and eliminated the offensive stipulations. The Displaced Persons laws, which ultimately allowed 410,-000 people into the United States, were so worded as to favor agriculturists, exiles from the Baltic ˹tates, and those of Germanic origin. In 1953 when the Displaced Persons Act expired, Congress enacted the Refugee Relief Act. Under it another 189,000 persons were admitted. Passed during the height of the cold war, the measure was meant to aid refugees as well as escapees from communist-dominated areas.

These additional bills only scratched the surface of the immigration problem. Postwar dislocations and the onset of the cold war exacerbated the difficulties of readjustment, and millions more still sought entry into the United States. To cope with the needs of these people, as well as to contain the voices of their friends and relatives in the United States who wanted to liberalize American immigration policies' Congress established a committee to look into the question. Under the chairmanship of Senator Patrick A. Mc-Carran of Nevada, an avowed opponent of leniency in immigration procedures, a subcommittee carefully studied the old laws and the mass of rules, regulations, and proclamations governing immigration. They gathered data, heard testimony from 400 persons and organizations, and then recommended that the basic national origins system remain intact. While rejecting theories of Nordic supremacy, the committee held, nonetheless, "that the peoples who made the greatest contribution to the development of this country were fully justified in determining that the country was no longer a field for further colonization and, henceforth, further immigration would not only be restricted but directed to admit immigrants considered to be more readily assimilable because of the similarity of their background to those of the principal components of our population." McCarran and his followers warned that "we have in the United States today hard-core, indigestible blocs which have not become integrated into the American way of life but which, on the contrary, are our deadly enemies." The proposed legislation, known as the McCarran-Walter Immigration Act of 1952, maintained the national origins system and provided a quota of 100 for all of those nations that did not have any quota allotment. In addition, the measure created preferences for skilled workers and relatives and strengthened security procedures. President Truman, who favored broadening the immigration laws and eliminating the offensive national origins quotas, rejected the bill, but Congress overrode his veto.

Within a few years after the McCarran-Walter Act had become law, efforts were made to modify it. Soon after the abortive Hungarian Revolution of 1956 Congress passed an act that admitted another 29,000 refugees, chiefly Hungarians, but also some Yugoslavians and Chinese. Some 31,000 Dutch-Indonesians, another uprooted group, came in under a law passed the next year. The United Nations declared 1960 World Refugee Year and Congress responded with the Fair Share Law, which opened the door to this country for a few more immigrants.

In addition to congressional actions, Presidents Eisenhower, Kennedy, and Johnson used the executive powers that they possessed under the existing immigration laws to relax restrictions. Thus, 30,000 Hungarians entered after 1956 as parolees without visas, ineligible for permanent alien registration until they had been here for two years. President Kennedy ordered the admission of thousands more, especially the Hong Kong Chinese and Cubans who sought refuge after Castro's seizure of power in 1959.

In 1963 President Kennedy urged Congress to eliminate the national origins system, which he insisted lacked "basis in either logic or reason. It neither satisfies a national need nor accomplishes an international purpose. In an age of interdependence among nations, such a system is an anachronism, for it discriminates among applicants for admission into the United States on the basis of the accident of birth." After President Kennedy's death President Johnson called upon Congress to enact the Kennedy proposal. Congress held extensive hearings and finally passed a new immigration bill overwhelmingly in 1965. Designed to be effective in 1968, the act abolished the national origins quota system and made other modifications in immigration policy.

Although the national origins proviso disappeared, an overall limitation remained. Outside of the Western Hemisphere only 170,000 persons, exclusive of parents, spouses, and children of American citizens, were to be allowed to enter the United States. No nation was permitted to have more than 20,000 of this total. Persons were admitted on a first-come–first-served basis under a system of preferences for the reunion of families, for refugees, and for professional, skilled, and unskilled workers needed in the economy.

The liberalization of the law for Asians and Europeans accompanied a shift in policy toward Canadians and Latin Americans. For the first time Congress placed a limit—120,000—on immigration from the Western Hemisphere. The administration had not pressed for this restriction, but a majority in Congress feared the possibility of a massive increase in Latin-American migrants.

The changing policies of postwar America led to an increase in immigration compared to the lean depression years. Whereas only 700,000 arrived in the 1930s and 120,000 during World War II, the numbers rose in the late 1940s. In 1950 nearly a quarter of a three years of the 1970s more than a million new arrivals came, and from 1961 to 1970 the figure reached 3,321,677. In the first three years of the 1970s more than a million new arrivals came, and there is the promise of an even greater increase.

Many of the refugees from World War II and from communism had great difficulty beginning life anew in America. They faced the usual problems of millions before them: language barriers, shortages of funds and skills, and the cultural shock of the new environment. Often there was the discouragement in finding a good job. "I knew I would have to start at the bottom of the employment ladder, but I had no idea that the bottom rung was so far underground," lamented a newcomer. Moreover, many of the displaced persons (DPs) had experienced the horrors of concentration-camp life, including malnutrition and physical torture, and this made adjustment still more difficult.

Yet these people had some advantages. Whether they were refugees fleeing from communism or those released from concentration or DP camps, the general climate was probably more friendly to the immigrants than it had been at any other time in modern American history. A host of private organizations and governmental agencies stood ready to assist them. Jewish groups that had actively assisted refugees in the 1930s continued their efforts. The United Service for New Americans, formed in 1946, was especially helpful to Jewish DPs. Various other European ethnic and religious groups also helped the newcomers. The federal government and some local governments assisted still others, and the federal government even airlifted some of those escaping from communism and provided emergency housing for them. In 1957 Hungarians fleeing after the Russian army had crushed the Hungarian Revolution were flown in and quartered temporarily at Camp Kilmer in New Jersey. A federal program begun in 1960 and implemented by the Department of Health, Education, and Welfare aided the Cuban refugees; later the department helped others such as the

Chinese. Often national and local governments and private agencies worked closely together to make the adjustment of the immigrant easier. Moreover, many refugees from communism found America sympathetic to their anti-communist views. By comparison, then, most of the newcomers probably experienced fewer problems than had the nineteenth- and early twentieth-century immigrants. They were fortunate, too, in coming during a period of relative prosperity after World War II, when jobs were available.

Although about 1 million came as refugees, most of the newcomers did not. They came for the usual reasons: to join families already here in America or to seek better opportunities. Whether from Mexico, Canada, or elsewhere in the Western Hemisphere or from Europe or more recently from Asia, a compelling reason for immigration has been an economic one. And a striking aspect of postwar emigration has been the growing numbers of professionals, especially scientists, engineers, and physicians, leaving their homes for America.

Most of the immigrants were not professionals. Nor, as had been customary in an earlier era, were a majority of those coming after World War II males. The War Brides Act, the refugee laws, and the provisions for uniting families helped tip the sex ratio in favor of women. Many immigrants were young children coming with their parents. Thus the bulk of the post–World War II entrants were not admitted under the category of general occupations. But of those who did have training, a larger proportion than ever before were professionals. In fact, by the 1960s professionals made up the largest percentage of those ranked occupationally, and in 1972 of the 167,241 immigrants with skills 48,887 (28 percent) were listed as professional, technical, and kindred workers.

From the end of the war until the late 1960s Great Britain and Canada, especially, sent scientists and engineers to America, and Germany was not far behind. The number of doctors emigrating to the United States also increased steadily. In 1949, 1,148 of them came, but in 1972 that figure was topped by India alone. Most of the immigrant scientists and engineers found jobs in private industry, but a considerable number taught and did research in American universities. Many of those emigrating had originally come with a temporary visa or as students but, after stays of varying periods, elected to remain in this country.

The scientific community of America was disproportionately foreign-born. In 1961 the foreign-born comprised about 5 percent of the American population but 24 percent of the members of the National Academy of Sciences. The National Register of Scientific and Technical Personnel estimated in 1970 that 8 percent of the nation's professional scientists were born and had received their secondary education abroad. Of the 43 American holders of Nobel prizes in physics and chemistry through 1964, 16 were of foreign origin. Of the 28 Americans receiving Nobel prizes in medicine and physiology, 8 were foreign-born.

The situation in medicine was similar as American hospitals increasingly became dependent upon immigrant physicians for their staffs. In 1950 only 5 percent of the new medical licenses were granted to foreign graduates, but by 1961 this figure reached 18 percent. Most, but not all, of these foreign-trained doctors were immigrants. Ten years later, more immigrant doctors came to America than were graduated that year by half of the nation's 120 medical schools. In New York City, where nearly 30 percent of the foreign-born doctors settled, 70 to 80 percent of the residents and interns of some hospitals were immigrants.

While the immigration laws and procedures favored the admission of scientists, engineers, and doctors from abroad, attractive conditions in America were also essential to lure them. A study done by the National Science Foundation in mid-1970 revealed several reasons for the emigration to America. Many, such as the Cubans, disliked their political situation at home, and others were curious about life in America. Insufficient opportunities for research at home also drove some out. But, above all, the existing opportunities still made the United States seem like the land of golden opportunity. Most of the newcomers cited a higher standard of living in America, lower taxes, and higher salaries as major factors inducing emigration. Ninety percent of the immigrant scientists and engineers made more than $10,000 annually, and 9 percent made more than $20,000. About one-half said that their American salary was at least 200 percent greater than it would have been at home.

The brain drain to the New World prompted uneasiness in several European nations and especially in Great Britain. A committee of the Royal Society concluded in 1963, "We have not been able to arrive at a reliable figure for the cost of educating these scientists. We regard as much more serious the economic conse-

Table 5-1.   Immigrants Born in Specified Countries and Areas: Years Ended
June 30, 1973 and 1965

Country of birth	Number		Percent change
	1973	1965	
Total immigrants	400,063	296,697	+ 34.8
Total Northern and Western Europe	24,548	73,318	− 66.5
Belgium	325	1,005	− 67.7
Denmark	428	1,384	− 69.1
France	1,845	4,039	− 54.3
Germany	6,600	24,045	− 72.6
Ireland	2,000	5,463	− 63.4
Netherlands	1,016	3,085	− 67.1
Norway	415	2,256	− 81.6
Sweden	573	2,411	− 76.2
Switzerland	577	1,984	− 70.9
United Kingdom	10,638	27,358	− 61.1
Other Northern and Western Europe	131	288	− 54.5
Total Southern and Eastern Europe	68,322	40,106	+ 70.4
Austria	528	1,680	− 68.6
Czechoslovakia	1,552	1,894	− 18.1
Greece	10,751	3,002	+ 258.1
Hungary	1,624	1,574	+ 3.2
Italy	22,151	10,821	+ 104.7
Poland	4,914	8,465	− 42.0
Portugal	10,751	2,005	+ 436.2
Romania	1,623	1,644	− 1.3
Spain	4,134	2,200	+ 87.9
U.S.S.R.	1,248	1,853	− 32.7
Yugoslavia	7,582	2,818	+ 169.1
Other Southern and Eastern Europe	1,464	2,150	− 31.9
Total Asia	124,160	20,683	+ 500.3
China & Taiwan	17,297	4,057	+ 326.3
Hong Kong	4,359	712	+ 512.2
India	13,124	582	+2,155.0
Iran	2,998	804	+ 272.9
Israel	1,917	882 ⸴	+ 117.3
Japan	5,461	3,180	+ 71.7
Jordan	2,450	702	+ 249.0
Korea	22,930	2,165	+ 959.1
Philippines	30,799	3,130	+ 884.0
Turkey	1,899	905	+ 109.8
Other Asia	20,926	3,564	+ 487.1

Table 5–1. Immigrants Born in Specified Countries and Areas: Years Ended June 30, 1973 and 1965 (continued)

Country of birth	Number		Percent change
	1973	1965	
Total North America	152,788	126,729	+ 20.6
Canada	8,951	38,327	− 76.7
Mexico	70,141	37,969	+ 84.7
West Indies	64,765	37,583	+ 72.3
Cuba	24,147	19,760	+ 22.2
Dominican Republic	13,921	9,504	+ 46.5
Haiti	4,786	3,609	+ 32.6
Jamaica	9,963	1,837	+ 442.4
Trinidad and Tobago	7,035	485	+1,350.5
Other West Indies	4,913	2,388	+ 105.7
Other North America	8,931	12,850	− 30.5
Total South America	20,335	30,962	− 34.3
Total Africa	6,655	3,383	+ 96.7
Total Oceania	3,255	1,512	+ 115.3
Other countries	−	4	−

SOURCE: Annual Report U.S. Immigration and Naturalization Service, 1973

quences of the loss to this country of the leadership and the creative contributions to science and technology which they would have made in the course of their working lives." Although the number coming from Great Britain was the largest from any one country, the drain was just as serious from the Netherlands, Norway, and Sweden. By 1968, however, partly because of improved conditions in Europe and the changes in the immigration laws, the brain drain from Europe to America declined while the numbers of Asian and Latin American scientists and engineers arriving in the United States increased.

The increase in the number of professionals from the developing nations was part of a general shift in immigration patterns largely prompted by the new immigration act of 1965. From 1965 until 1973 immigration increased from 296,697 to 400,063. But marked shifts occurred as can be seen from Table 5-1. In 1965 the numbers coming from northern and western Europe outnumbered those coming from eastern and southern Europe, but the situation reversed itself by 1973, with large decreases for Great

Britain and Germany and large increases from Greece, Italy, and Portugal. Emigrants from Jamaica, Trinidad, and Tobago in the Western Hemisphere also contributed to the expanding American figures. But the biggest increases in immigration were from Asia. In 1965 only about 7 percent of the immigrants arrived from the Far East. By 1973 there were 124,160, or about 32 percent of the total. Outside the Western Hemisphere the largest number of immigrants of any nation in 1973 were from the Philippines (30,799), followed by Korea (22,930), and then by Italy (22,151), and the Asian nations of China and Taiwan (17,297), and India (13,124).

The numbers of these recent immigrants were not large compared to the turn-of-the-century immigration, but they had great impact. In recent years, and especially since the passage of the immigration act of 1965, Filipino immigration to the United States has increased both to the mainland and Hawaii. Over 30,000 came in 1973. In the early 1970s the Filipino community in Honolulu and environs was the largest in the world outside of the Philippine Islands and numbered over 60,000. Like other Asians, many of the recent immigrants have been professional workers. A large contingent found itself stigmatized on the West Coast but not on the East Coast. As a result, many of the better-educated Filipinos have come to New York. It was estimated that in 1973 there were more Filipino doctors in America than black ones, and there is hardly a hospital in San Francisco, Los Angeles, or Chicago without Filipino nurses.

The changed immigration laws have affected other Asians also. From 1951 to 1960 only 25,201 persons, mostly Chinese, entered America from China, Taiwan and Hong Kong. From 1961 to 1973, however, the figure rose to 162,052. The impact of such immigration was potentially staggering when one realizes the Chinese-American population during the same time was less than 400,000. Moreover, Chinese Americans were generally concentrated in Chinatowns of a few American cities, such as San Francisco, New York, and Honolulu. The immigrants headed for these cities and substantially swelled the Chinese-American populations already there. San Francisco's Chinatown grew from 30,000 in 1952 to an estimated 65,000 in 1972. The rapid influx of immigrants strained housing, job, and community facilities; and in the early 1970s newspapers carried stories of conflicts between the old and new Chinese, including violent gang and street fights. The nation's Chinatowns had won a reputation for their low crime rates, but it was now threatened by the new violence.

Like earlier immigrants without language and labor skills, Chinese immigrants could be exploited. Even when they had mastered English, they had trouble finding work. One Chinese described his parents' situation in a garment factory: "There [are] no vacations, no pensions; they just work and work all their lives. We're willing to work, but can't find [good] jobs." In 1972 an estimated 7,500 Chinese, most of whom were immigrants and many of whom were women, worked in 250 garment factories—virtual sweatshops in New York City's Chinatown—for wages as low as 65 and 75 cents an hour. A Labor Department administrator said these "employees in Chinatown are one of the worst exploited groups in the metropolitan area."

The 1965 immigration law also led to the entrance of groups like Indians from Asia, who formed one colony in Hoboken, New Jersey, and Haitians from the Caribbean. There had been Haitians in the United States for years, but sharp increases in new arrivals in the past decade augmented their community. These French-speaking immigrants fled the dictatorial regime of François Duvalier and a severely depressed economy. Once in the United States, they took whatever jobs they could get, which often paid poorly. They suffered because they were blacks as well as immigrants. Like other newcomers before them, they congregated together, and one Haitian colony, as their ghetto in the Crown Heights section of Brooklyn is called, already had about 75,000 people by the early 1970s.

In retrospect the past half-century seems to have witnessed a major transformation in the sources of American immigration. The bulk of Europeans were primarily political refugees or DPs, like the Jews who escaped from Hitler or the Hungarians who fled after the 1956 revolution or skilled and professional workers. These newer immigrants, mostly of middle-class origin, had an easier time being accepted and adjusting to the standards of American life. The 1965 immigration law, furthermore, requires that preference be given to close relatives and those whose skills are in greatest demand in this country. Members of both of these categories will certainly have more assistance establishing themselves in the United States than had those who disembarked friendless and bewildered, 75 or 100 years ago.

The most noticeable new groups in the United States are now the Spanish-speaking minorities. Driven out of their homelands by deeply rooted poverty, a revolution of rising expectations in Latin America, and, on occasion, by political changes at home and drawn to the United States by cheap and fast transportation and a seeming abundance of low-skilled jobs on American farms and in the larger cities, these people are making a significant impact on our society. They are important enough to be the subject of the next chapter.

Chapter 6

The Spanish-Speaking
Minorities

The past half-century has been the era of the Spanish-speaking minorities in the United States. Most of the Europeans and Asians who have arrived in the past three or four decades have found it relatively easy to fit into American society. Their period of adjustment took only a few years, and with the exception of groups like the Chinese in crowded Chinatowns and perhaps the Portuguese in New Bedford, Massachusetts, they were rarely visible in society as immigrant or minority groups. For the Spanish speaking, who have been plagued by low incomes, poor housing, and discrimination, this has not usually been the case.

So great has been the movement to America from Latin America that the census records of March 1973 revealed that there were more than 10 million people of Mexican, Puerto Rican, Cuban, and other Spanish-speaking origins in this country. The figure was surely understated because many who have arrived illegally have not been counted by the federal government. The Spanish-speaking peoples are, after the black Americans, the nation's largest minority, and some governmental officials estimate that within a generation the Latin communities in the United States may outnumber those of the blacks. "The implications for this country are enormous," declared Henry M. Ramirez, chairman of the federal Cabinet Committee on Opportunities for Spanish-Speaking People. He concluded: "Not too far in the future, many areas will have Spanish-speaking majorities, and Latin American culture will make a very deep impression on the mainstream of U.S. society."

The signs of the Spanish vitality were evident almost everywhere in America and not only in utterances of governmental officials and census data. More than 100 television and radio stations broadcast their programs in Spanish, and shops from California to New York display *"Aquí se habla español"* placards in their windows. New York was well known for its Puerto Rican flavor, Los Angeles for its Mexican influence, and Miami for its "Little Havana," but even cities like San Antonio, Denver, Kansas City, Chicago, and Philadephia also have their Spanish-speaking contingents.

Of the Spanish-speaking those of Mexican origin total 6.3 million, 80 percent of whom live in the Southwest, and the majority of those people live in urban areas. They constitute approximately 16 percent of the population in California, 18 percent in Texas, 40 percent in New Mexico, 19 percent in Arizona, and 13 percent in Colorado. The Los Angeles area alone has more than 1 million people of Mexican ancestry and, except for Mexico City, is the largest Mexican city in the world. In addition, it is estimated that there are about 300,000 or more Mexicans in the Chicago area and smaller colonies in Detroit, Kansas City (Missouri), and other places in the Midwest. Those of Puerto Rican background total almost 1.5 million, with the majority living in the New York City area. There are smaller concentrations of Puerto Ricans in Chicago, Philadelphia, Miami, and cities in New Jersey and Connecticut. Southern Florida contains about half of the nation's 750,000 Cubans, most of whom have arrived since Fidel Castro became Cuban premier in 1959. Other Cubans are scattered throughout the country, but more than 75,000 live in New York City and environs. New York City also has colonies of other Latin Americans, many of whom entered this country illegally; but census records have not delineated their numbers.

The Mexican Americans are the largest and most prominent of the Spanish-speaking group and, after the blacks, are the single largest minority group in the United States. Until about 10 or 15 years ago they were a forgotten minority, but in more recent times historians, sociologists, journalists, politicians, and governmental officials have become increasingly aware of their presence. Moreover, in the same period there have arisen four prominent Mexican-American leaders—César Chavez, Reies López Tijerina, Rudolpho "Corky" González and José Angel Guitierrez.

Some Mexicans in the United States, especially those in New Mexico and southern Colorado, can trace their ancestry back many centuries. The city of Santa Fe, New Mexico, was founded in 1609, a generation before the Puritans set foot in New England. Most of what is now the heartland of Mexican-American country in the five states of the Southwest belonged to Spain and then to Mexico; the United States did not annex it until the signing of the Treaty of Guadalupe Hidalgo in 1848. At that time Mexico recognized the American annexation of Texas, and she also ceded all or part of what is now present-day Colorado, New Mexico, Nevada, Arizona, and California. Aside from Nevada all of these states now have important Mexican-American communities. In the treaty of Guadalupe Hidalgo the United States guaranteed that all of the Mexican citizens in the newly acquired territories would be able to retain their property and traditions. Those who chose not to leave within a year were accorded American citizenship with all of its rights and privileges. It is estimated that the Mexican population of the Southwest at that time was about 75,000, with most of the settlements in what is now New Mexico and California.

Ever since, the history of the Mexicans in the United States has been tied to the history of the Southwest. As the region grew, so did the influx of Mexicans—legal and illegal, permanent and temporary, daily and seasonal commuter, student and tourist. The beginning of the twentieth century witnessed the completion of the great southwestern railroads, the expansion of cotton planting in Texas, Arizona, and California, and the irrigation of farmlands in the Imperial and San Joaquin valleys in California. All of these industries needed plentiful cheap labor, and the Mexican worker provided it. As the century progressed, Mexicans provided more than 60 percent of the common laborers on the railroad-track gangs, in the mines of Arizona and New Mexico, for the fruit and truck crops of Texas and California, and in the numerous packing plants on the West Coast. They also dominated the labor supply in the sugar-beet fields of Colorado and cultivated sugar beets in states as far north as Montana and Michigan and as far east as Ohio.

The coming of Mexican laborers coincided not only with the rapid growth and development of the Southwest but also with the curbing of immigration from China and Japan and later from Europe and with the revolutionary upheavals in Mexico beginning in 1910. Mexican workers, cowboys, shepherds, and ranch hands had crossed the Mexican-American border frequently and easily between 1850 and 1910 just as others had moved north and south or east and west in the United States. There was no border patrol, and American immigration officials were more concerned about keeping out Orientals than with tracking down small numbers of Mexicans. But the growth of agriculture demanded hundreds of thousands of cheap, mobile laborers who could pick the crops quickly and then perhaps move on to other areas and harvest whatever else was ripe. In Texas the migratory farmers usually started in the southern part of the state in June, then moved eastward and eventually went west for the later harvest in the central part of the state. In California, on the other hand (where more than 200 crops are cultivated), the growing season ranges from 240 to 365 days, thereby keeping workers busy all year. Today that state's agricultural income alone exceeds $4 billion annually.

Before 1910 most of the Mexican migrants were temporary laborers, but after the upheaval caused by the Mexican Revolution many permanent settlers arrived. Although the overwhelming number were lower-class agrarian workers, the migration also included artisans, professionals, and businessmen whose property was destroyed by the violence accompanying the revolutionary chaos.

The Mexican Revolution spurred movement but so too did a number of other factors. From 1877 to 1910 Mexico's population increased from 9.4 million to 15 million without a commensurate increase in the means of subsistence. A small percentage of *hacendados* (feudal barons) controlled most of the country's land, which was tilled by the agricultural proletariat. There existed between hacienda owners and their laborers a patron-peon relationship, and each behaved according to well-defined roles. As the economy boomed, though, prices rose while daily wages remained constant or even declined to an amount well below that needed to care for a family. At the beginning of the twentieth century, however, the construction of the Mexican Central and Mexican National railroads, as well as the opening of mines in northern Mexico, encouraged movement. Once the exodus from central and eastern Mexico began, many workers saw no need to stop at the border. Wages in the United States were at least five times as much as in Mexico, and American businessmen avidly sought the foreign peon. As two scholars who have studied the Mexican migration have pointed out, the inability of the Mexicans "to speak English, their ignorance of personal rights under American law, and their recent experience as virtual serfs under the exploitative dictatorship of Porfirio Díaz made them ideal workers from the growers' viewpoint." The northward migration brought about 10 percent of Mexico's population to the southwestern borderlands.

The first Mexican migrants in the twentieth century were overwhelmingly males, mostly transient, who found work on the railroad-track gangs. They lived in boxcars and moved from place to place with railroads such as the Southern Pacific, the Santa Fe, and the Chicago, Rock Island and Pacific. By 1910 they could be found from Chicago to California and as far north as Wyoming. They were cheap laborers who worked for $1 to $1.25 a day, less than their predecessors—the Greeks, the Italians, and the Japanese. Many of today's Mexican-American *colonias* (settlements) originated as railroad labor camps.

With the influx of Mexicans into the United States, El Paso developed as a major placement center and assembly point for workers in an arc reaching from Louisiana to the state of Washington. Three major railroads passed through this border city, and not only were railroad, mine, and seasonal agricultural workers recruited here, but representatives from labor-contracting companies also took thousands of immigrants to distributing centers in Kansas City (Missouri), Los Angeles, and San Antonio.

After 1910 more and more of the Mexican newcomers found work in agriculture rather than on the railroads. This was true despite the fact that the major southwestern railroad employed more than 50,000 Mexicans. During World War I, European immigration fell drastically, American residents went off to war, and the expanding agricultural acres needed hands. As a result the contract-labor laws were temporarily suspended in 1917, and Mexicans, otherwise ineligible for immigration visas, were brought in to cultivate the crops and work the harvest. The depression of 1921–1922 left many of them unemployed, but then the resumption of prosperity and the immigration restriction acts of 1921 and 1924 stimulated a further demand for Mexican labor. Large southwestern agricultural growers put great pressure on Congress to exempt Mexicans from the quota area, and their intensive efforts succeeded. Before 1965, though, to be legally admitted to the United States Mexicans had to pay fees for visas and medical examinations, show that they were literate and not likely to become public charges, and prove that they had not been guilty of violating the contract-labor laws. It is for these reasons, plus the fact that the border was so inadequately patrolled (not until 1924, in fact, was money appropriated for border wardens) that the Mexican agricultural workers found it easier simply to enter illegally than to go through the rigamarole of formal application. Scholars estimate that in the 1920s there were as many, if not more, illegal immigrants than there were legal ones—about 500,000. The 1920s immigrants worked primarily in the agricultural areas of California and Texas but also in the Michigan sugar-beet fields and in the industrial areas in and around Chicago, Detroit, Milwaukee, and western Pennsylvania. Chicago's Mexican population, in fact, shot up from 3,854 in 1920 to 19,362 ten years later, and the city claimed the largest Mexican population east of Denver.

The depression of the 1930s not only curtailed Mexican immigration, but many Mexicans and their American-born children were encouraged—often forced—by local governmental officials to return to Mexico, which was not seriously affected by the depression. The Mexican government he'ped many repatriates return; in some American cities like Los Angeles, however, welfare agencies paid for the return passage. It is estimated that almost half a million, or more than one-third of the Mexican-American population in 1930, was removed between 1929 and 1940. About half of these people were American-born.

The Mexicans who remained in the United States experienced severe deprivations. In Gary, Indiana, social workers found them living without furniture and with only a box for a table and the floor for a bed. Moreover, they were victimized by epidemics of tuberculosis and rickets, and malnutrition was common among Mexican children. One report, noting the poor housing, the large number of unemployed, and their deteriorating health, observed, "The agony and suffering that all of these people endure is beyond comprehension of any who have not experienced it." Through the Southwest agricultural wages fell from 35 cents to 15 cents an hour. In Texas Mexican cotton pickers, working from sunrise to sunset, were lucky to earn 80 cents a day, while other Mexican farm workers had to be content with 60 cents a day. In California by the late 1930s migratory Mexican families averaged $254 a year, and even there American whites were given preferential treatment. By 1939, in fact, more than 90 percent of the Golden State's field workers were dust-bowl refugees who had replaced the minority group members. In 1940 one investigator found that most of the Mexican agricultural workers in Hidalgo Country, Texas, earned less than $400 a year. In the same year it was found that a quarter of the Mexican children between 6 and 9 years of age worked in the fields with their parents, while 80 percent of those in the 10-to-14 age group did so as well.

The coming of World War II opened up new opportunities for the Mexican laborers in the Southwest. Many of those in California and Texas moved out of rural areas to urban centers, where they found jobs in airplane plants, shipyards, and other war-related industries. In the Midwest, steel mills, foundries, and automobile factories (which were now manufacturing for military needs) could not fill their job vacancies fast enough as those eligible for military service went off to war. The southwestern agricultural fields were also starved for workers.

At this juncture the governments of Mexico and the United States inaugurated an entirely new program—the importation of contract laborers, known as braceros, to work in the fields and on the railroads. According to the bracero agreement, Mexicans came into the United States for temporary, seasonal jobs then returned to Mexico when their tasks were completed. From 1942 to 1947, when the initial program ended, the United States received about 220,000 braceros. The program was administered by the United States Department of Agriculture, and the agreement stipulated that there would be a minimum number of guaranteed working days, adequate wages, and suitable living accommodations. Braceros worked in 21 states, with more than half going to California. The Mexican government would not allow any of its nationals to work in Texas, though, because of the intense discrimination that existed in the Lone Star State.

From the bracero's point of view the program was a good one. Most of the workers were men who could not provide adequately for their families at home, and the job opportunities in the United States offered what they considered good wages. Although they earned only 30 cents an hour and less than $500 a year, this amount still provided them with enough to send money back to their families.

Although protective provisions had been written into the law, many observers were later appalled to find the braceros living in converted chicken coops, abandoned railroad cars, and rickety wooden structures almost on the verge of collapsing. The braceros themselves, however, were attracted by the higher wages in the

United States and kept returning whenever they could. Their acceptance of conditions that many others would consider deplorable and degrading has been explained by Richard B. Craig in *The Bracero Program.* The Mexican laborer, Craig noted, is "a somewhat unique personality type; one accustomed to living, and indeed thriving, in a virtual state of physical and mental peonage. The Mexican . . . bracero or wetback* probably found little except language (and not always that) to distinguish between the *patron* and the strawboss. It would appear, in sum, that the sociopsychological milieu in which the average Mexican peasant was reared prepared him ideally for his role as the servile, hard-working, seldom complaining, perpetually polite bracero."

The original bracero program ended in 1947, but there were temporary extensions until 1951 when the clamorings from southwestern growers and the impact of the Korean War combined to induce Congress to reestablish it. The second time it lasted until 1964. Table 6-1 shows the numbers of braceros entering the United

Table 6–1. *Braceros* Entering the U.S. Under Contract, 1942–1964

1942	4,203	1950	67,500	1958	432,857
1943	52,098	1951	192,000	1959	437,643
1944	62,170	1952	197,100	1960	315,846
1945	49,454	1953	201,388	1961	291,420
1946	32,043	1954	309,033	1962	194,978
1947	19,632	1955	398,650	1963	186,865
1948	35,345	1956	445,197	1964	177,736
1949	107,000	1957	436,049		

SOURCE: Ralph Guzman, Leo Grebler, and Joan W. Moore, *The Mexican-American People* (New York: The Free Press, 1970), p. 68. Reprinted by permission.

States during the 22-year program. The apparently bottomless reservoir of cheap labor from south of the border helped build up the multibillion-dollar agricultural concerns from California through Texas, which, unlike the wartime years, were now included in the revised program. One appreciative and callous grower acknowledged: "We used to own slaves but now we rent them from the government."

* The term "wetback" (*mojado*), which designates an illegal immigrant, originated because many Mexicans waded across the Rio Grande River, which separates Mexico from Texas, during relatively dry periods when the water was shallow.

In the 1950s braceros earned 50 cents an hour (30 cents cotton chopping in Arkansas) and undercut American laborers. The Mexican Americans in the Southwest were particularly resentful. They did the same work as the braceros, often side by side, but for lower wages, worse housing and facilities, and with no provision for transportation. The humiliation and bitterness that these citizens felt when they compared their situation to that of the imported foreign laborers eventually reached the ears of liberal politicians in Congress and prominent labor officials. Both groups protested the continued maintenance of the bracero program, but they lacked either the numbers or the influence to prevail in the 1950s. In the 1960s the Kennedy administration proved more sympathetic and helped provide for the program's demise. Other factors also militated against the program. The southwestern growers had already begun to increase mechanization and thereby decreased their need for more hands; in 1962 Secretary of Labor Arthur Goldberg imposed a $1-an-hour minimum wage; and at about the same time, labor shortages below the Rio Grande made the Mexican government anxious to curb the agreements. These factors combined to kill the bracero program. During the 22 years of its existence, though, from 1942 to 1964, almost 5 million braceros came into the country, and they were viewed, literally, as an annual miracle indispensable to the southwestern economy. Moreover, their earnings contributed to the Mexican economy as well, because they sent more than $200 million to their relatives at home.

Besides braceros, whose wages and living conditions were stipulated by agreement, the southwestern farmers also employed an untold number of wetbacks, or illegal immigrants. The wetbacks were often those who for one reason or another were not selected by the Mexican government for the bracero program but whose backgrounds and needs were often similar to those who were admitted. The conditions wetbacks were willing to accept in the United States—wages of 20 to 30 cents an hour, housing without plumbing or electricity, washing in irrigation ditches—indicate how appalling life must have been in Mexico. Certainly, the inhumanity and cruelty that they experienced here must have been an improvement over what they left behind; otherwise they would not have struggled so to enter the United States. The growers, of course, found them ideal laborers. Fearing disclosure of their illegal status, the Mexicans performed their tasks well; they neither argued nor complained, and they cost practically nothing. In fact, some un-scrupulous southwestern farmers turned in their wetbacks to immigration officials before payday, thereby saving themselves the meager cost of their workers' wages. Between 1947 and 1954, when the Immigration Service inaugurated a major campaign to round up and deport illegal aliens, more than 4 million wetbacks were apprehended in the United States, but no one knows how many escaped detection by authorities. Between 1946 and 1954, however, they were the single most important source of southwestern farm labor.

That the Mexicans and Mexican Americans were victimized and exploited there can be no doubt. But why they apparently endured such abuse for so many decades with scarcely any major protests until the 1960s requires a deeper inquiry into their backgrounds. The Mexican Americans of the Southwest, a product of several centuries of intermixture between Spaniards and Indians, come from a culture of poverty and discrimination. For generations, in both Mexico and this country, they had been forced to assume the lowest position in the social order. The Roman Catholic Church, which in Mexico combines traditional doctrine with native folk practices, preached a certain fatalism about life, and the relationship of the rural poor to the major landowners, or patrons, reinforced these teachings. Education for the peons in Mexico prior to 1930 was practically nonexistent, and they came to regard it as a luxury for the upper classes. The immigrants brought such attitudes with them to the United States, and this, combined with the prejudices and inadequacies of schoolteachers and administrators ill prepared to handle Spanish-speaking children, has prevented Mexican children from exploiting educational opportunities in the ways that Jewish, German, Greek, Armenian, and Oriental children have. Finally, it must also be noted that many of the Mexican workers looked upon their years in the United States as a temporary expedient. They expected to return home; their sojourn north of the border more likely than not gave them an improved status in their home communities. As one Mexican newspaper explained it, in the United States these workers "learn many good things, to be temperate, to dress well, to earn good wages, to live properly, to eat properly, to speak English and much of modern agriculture. That is, they become cultured and when they return to Mexico, they progress rapidly."

The Mexican peasants who moved to the United States may

have crossed an international boundary, but, for the most part, they continued to dwell in a land whose physical characteristics were familiar and among people who might easily have been their neighbors at home. The Mexican communities in the Southwest, for example, were so well developed that the newcomer did not have to change his faith, alter his language, or relinquish other cultural ties in order to be accepted. Continued migrations sustained these Mexican *colonias* in the United States and to a considerable extent retarded assimilation and acculturation.

In this country the large farmers and industrialists welcomed the Mexican for the labor that he provided. Lack of familiarity with Mexican customs allowed the Americans to misinterpret good manners and respect for authority as docility, illiteracy for ignorance, and a lack of the Puritan work ethic for laziness. Moreover, the fact that good jobs were scarce and that illegal entry compromised a man's position also precluded Mexican bitterness and anger from surfacing at the wrong moments.

That Mexicans were docile is belied by their history in the past century. In Mexico the revolution of 1910 was, at least in part, a peasant movement, and in the United States too there were enough incidents of labor strife to call for a reexamination of careless characterizations. Mexicans led strikes in the Texas Panhandle in 1883 and on the Pacific Railways in Los Angeles 20 years later. To protest labor conditions thousands of Mexican workers walked away from sugar-beet, onion, celery, berry, and citrus crops in California, Texas, Idaho, Colorado, Washington, and Michigan in the 1920s and 1930s. That these protests produced few permanent advances does not reflect defects in the Mexican character, but rather the harshness of reprisals, the intense competition for jobs, the shifting nature of the work force (migrant workers), the mechanization of agriculture, and the movement of the more prosperous and accomplished to urban areas where industrial opportunities promised greater remuneration.

Another problem that Mexicans and other minorities have had in the United States is that Americans could not or would not understand why any group was reluctant to part with its own heritage and to embrace quickly the values of the dominant society. But the fact was that the Mexican peon struggled from day to day merely to provide the essentials of life for his family. He often did not see the long-range benefits that might accrue to his children from a good education. Even when he did, he may have been shrewd enough to recognize that American education would undermine traditional values and lead his children away from the family and its culture and into the outstretched arms of the dominant culture. Even in rural Mexico in the 1930s schools were built faster than students could be found to occupy them. The peasant was not enthusiastic about educating his children, for he cherished family life, in which everyone had a prescribed role. The status quo provided too much comfort and security for him to sacrifice it for another culture whose values he had difficulty comprehending.

Given Mexican-American resistance to acculturation, which was constantly reinforced by the physical proximity of the Mexican border, and given the continued influx of newcomers from the old country, it is not surprising that as late as the census of 1940 most Mexican-American families still spoke Spanish at home. Many of these families also looked upon their stay in the United States as a temporary one and expected to return to Mexico someday. With this pervasive frame of reference it is understandable why few broke away from their cultural patterns to seek a new way of life in the Anglo world. For those who attempted to do so, the intensity of societal prejudices made the leap almost insuperable.

Although discrimination against Mexicans existed throughout the American Southwest, it was not uniform in either emotional tone or effect. For example, Mexicans were expected to live in their own barrios (ghettos), were restricted from many public recreational facilities, could obtain mostly menial and relatively unskilled jobs, and, in general, were expected to accept a subordinate role in society. In New Mexico, however, there was a tradition of Hispanic participation in government, and the upper-class Americans of Mexican background moved easily throughout society. In New Mexico, also, those of Mexican descent, regardless of class, have been active in local politics, and their numbers (until recently almost half of the population) have determined where and when they could hold office. In Colorado Mexican *colonias* date back to the 1850s, and there, too, prejudice existed but was not intense. Nor was Arizona, despite its segregated schools and movie theatres, a particularly harsh place for Mexicans. But in California, and especially in Texas, bigotry toward Mexicans has been extreme. In the Lone Star State, with its strong Southern heritage, Mexicans encountered more overt discrimination than anywhere else in the country. Food shops routinely refused service to those of Mexican ancestry; teachers called children greasers in kindergarten; and many churches held separate services "For Colored and Mexicans." Typical of the attitudes of many whites was this statement from a Texas farmer. "You can't mix with a Mexican and hold his respect," he told an interviewer. "It's like the nigger; as long as you keep him in his place he is all right." And during World War II, when the Mexican government, incensed at the treatment those of Mexican ancestry received in Texas, refused to allow braceros to work in the state, one Mexican-American weekly noted: "The Nazis of Texas are not political partners of the Fuhrer of Germany but indeed they are slaves to the same prejudices and superstitions."

It was also during World War II when two particularly heinous events involving Mexican Americans took place in Los Angeles. One, in 1942, involved the arrest and conviction of a gang of teenage boys for murder although the prosecution presented no evidence at the trial to justify their conviction. Existing community prejudices, however, combined with the unkempt and disheveled appearances of the youths (the prosecuting attorney refused to allow them to bathe or change their clothes during the first week of the trial) sufficed to bring forth a guilty verdict. Similar miscarriages of justice reflecting community prejudices have been rendered in other sections of the country toward other minority group members at different times, but few have been marked by such gross disregard of evidence. Inability to raise bail forced the defendants to spend two years in San Quentin prison before an appeals court unanimously reversed the lower court's decision "for lack of evidence" and reprimanded the trial judge for his injudicious behavior during the proceedings.

The other event that won national attention and pitted Mexican-American youths against Anglos took place in June 1943. The Zoot Suit Riots involved Mexican-American youth sporting the then faddish zoot suit of baggy trousers with high waists and tight cuffs, long coats with wide shoulders and loose backs, and broad-brimmed flat hats. On the evening of June 3, 1943, a group of sailors were assaulted while walking in a slum area surrounded by the Mexican barrio. The sailors claimed that their assailants were Mexicans. They reported the incident to the police, who returned to the area but could find no one to arrest. The following night 200 sailors took the law into their own hands, went into the Mexican district of Los

Angeles, and beat up every zoot suiter they could find. One naval officer explained their mission: "We're out to do what the police have failed to do, we're going to clean up this situation. . . ." Not surprisingly, the Los Angeles police at the time did nothing to deter the servicemen from their course. For the next few nights sailors, soldiers, and marines paraded the streets of Los Angeles indiscriminately attacking Mexicans in what *Time* magazine called "the ugliest brand of mob action since the coolie race riots of the 1870s." It took the intervention of the Mexican government through the United States Department of State to curb military leaves in the Los Angeles area, which thereby resulted in a cessation of this mob action. The Zoot Suit Riots led to the formation of the Los Angeles Commission on Human Rights in 1944, but the new organization could do little to alter established prejudices.

In retrospect it is difficult to imagine positive effects emerging from, on the one hand, a miscarriage of justice and, on the other, a bloody riot; yet the two events did at least focus attention upon the Mexican Americans in an urban setting. Most writing about Mexican Americans portrays them as living in rural areas and as being exploited by money-hungry large scale growers. While this picture is not totally unfounded, after World War II only the Mexican-American minority, not the majority, was still tied to the land. In 1950 two-thirds of those of Mexican ancestry lived in urban areas; and today about 85 percent of the Mexican Americans live in American cities.

In an urban setting Mexican Americans have come to resemble other immigrants and minorities in American history. The second and third generations are beginning to break away from familiar traditions and place more of an emphasis on American values. The extended family has been gradually replaced by the more typically American nuclear family, and work horizons have expanded. During World War II, when opportunities developed in airplane plants and shipyards, the urbanized Mexican did not have to leave at harvest time to earn more money in the field. After the war there were additional opportunities. By the 1950s Mexican Americans made up 20 percent of California's auto workers, half of the members of the building-trades union, and a majority of those working in the state's garment factories.

Semiskilled and skilled jobs had opened up opportunities for advancement and assimilation for many minorities, and they did so for the Mexicans also. By 1970 more than 30,000 people of Mexican ancestry held professional positions, and although their enrollment in colleges and universities was still small, it was growing nonetheless. Training and opportunities will no doubt accelerate the pace of assimilation and, as a concomitant, force the relinquishment of some traditional Mexican-American values.

In spite of these efforts at assimilation and advancement, it must still be emphasized that as a group the Mexican Americans, although comparatively well off in the urban areas of California today, still constitute one-third of those below the poverty level in Texas and New Mexico and one-fourth of the poor in Arizona and Colorado. The median annual income for Mexican-American families in 1972 was $8,759, higher than the $6,864 for blacks but lower than the $11,549 for Anglos. Rural Mexican-American families, such as those in northern New Mexico and southern Texas, however, have average yearly incomes of only about $2,300 and still live in shacks, often without plumbing or electricity. Both rural and urban Mexican Americans have fewer years of schooling than either blacks or Anglos and as a consequence will have a more difficult time in obtaining well-paying jobs and moving up the socioeconomic ladder, which is still considered the mark of success in America.

The existing deprivations, which Anglos have been willing to overlook or ascribe to inherent defects among those of Mexican descent, have given rise in the past decade to the development of an activist Chicano movement dedicated to improving the economic lot of the group while fostering a self-conscious nationalism. The Chicano activists arose in the late 1960s at a time when other frustrated groups like the blacks, Indians, and women were also vigorous in protesting their positions in American society. The Chicanos want to retain their ethnic identity while raising the standard of living of all Mexican Americans. Although they treasure the traditional values of their culture, including a respect and affection for the family, the cult of masculinity (*machismo*), and a sense of obligation to others in the community, their demands for equal education, training, and job opportunities will eventually produce Americans of Mexican descent and the Chicano movement will probably fade out.

Reflecting the goals of this emerging group are four prominent Mexican-American leaders whose basic commitment is to end the existing inequalities in American society. The best known of the four is César Chavez, who, along with 600 Filipinos and Filipino organizer Larry Itliong, led the California grape pickers on a five-year strike that ended with the strikers' receiving higher wages and improved working conditions in 1970. However, Chavez's union lost contracts and workers to the Teamsters Union in 1973 and 1974. On the surface Chavez's goals for the California farm workers appear to be the most limited of those of the four activists, but he was the first Chicano leader to achieve national prominence, and he has become both a symbol and a unifying force for Chicano aspirations.

In New Mexico Reies López Tijerina inaugurated the Alianza Federal de Mercedes (the Federal Alliance of Land Grants) in 1963 to regain for the Mexican Americans the lands that he charges Anglos stole from the ancestors of Mexican Americans in violation of the Treaty of Guadalupe Hidalgo. In this goal he has been unsuccessful, but like Chavez, he has been able to use this forum to focus on the state's rural poverty and also to rally those who believe in the Chicano movement. The zealousness of Tijerina and some of his followers has led them to massive acts of civil disobedience and a two-year prison term for the Alianza leader. Tijerina was released from jail in 1971 on condition that he hold no formal position in the Alianza movement.

In Denver, Colorado, and Crystal City in southeast Texas two other Chicano leaders have used more orthodox methods to rally their followers. Both started new political parties. In Denver in 1965 Rudolpho "Corky" González organized a civil rights group, which he hoped would develop into a new political party, known as the Crusade for Justice. The new organization dedicated itself to protecting individual Chicanos from police brutality and judicial bigotry while improving educational, occupational, and social conditions. In Texas, José Angel Guitierrez, following along the lines of González's Crusade for Justice, founded *La Raza Unida* party, which he hoped would result in Chicano control of some 20 counties where Mexican Americans constitute a majority in south Texas. Guitierrez believes that Chicanos can never control their own destinies or achieve political power by working within this country's major political parties.

These four men—indigenous leaders who have rallied and directed Mexican-American youth—have given Mexican Americans a new hope for the future. Within the past decade a whole flock of new organizations and groups like the Brown Berets and the Mexican-American Youth Organization (MAYO) have developed, including a Congress of Mexican-American Unity representing 200 different Chicano organizations, all dedicated to fostering the goals that the four major leaders have articulated so well. Their very presence suggests that the future for Americans of Mexican descent will be considerably different from the past.

Perhaps the most overlooked Spanish minority group is the Basques who settled in the Great Basin (the area roughly between Salt Lake City and the Sierra Nevada Mountains in east California, which includes most of Nevada, southeastern Oregon, and southwestern Idaho) at the end of the nineteenth and the beginning of the twentieth centuries. Their original homeland, Basque country on the Iberian peninsula in Europe, was taken over partially by France in 1789 but mainly by Spain in 1839. Since the Basque families, generation after generation, produced larger families than the local economy could absorb, grown children frequently emigrated. There are a number of Basques in many of the Latin American countries, and Basques also populated California during the Spanish and Mexican periods. Today, Boise, Idaho, houses the largest Basque contingent outside of the Iberian peninsula. Other Basque colonies are in eastern Oregon, California, Nevada, Wyoming, and Colorado. Since the Basques are Caucasians, they have not been enumerated separately in either immigration figures or census returns. One scholar estimates in 1970 that there were about 12,000 to 15,000 Basques, including members of the second and third generations, in the Idaho-Oregon area. It is unlikely that the entire Basque population in this country exceeds this figure; with intermarriage occurring it might even be less.

Historically, the Basques have been associated with the sheep industry in the West's Great Basin. They have been herders, foremen, buyers, transporters, and ranch owners. When they first arrived in the 1870s and 1880s, they were valued for their shepherding skills but despised as a minority. Some people referred to them derogatively as "Bascos," likened them to "Chinamen," and cruelly described them as filthy, treacherous, and meddlesome. Nevertheless, they maintained their calm and went about their work. Shepherding is a lonely, monotonous task, but the Basques excelled at it. Their culture values people who succeed in physically arduous tasks that also require grit and determination. One analyst opined that the Basque "sees physical labor and adverse working conditions as a personal challenge which affords an opportunity to merit the approbation of his peers." The Basques dominated the Western sheep industry from the end of the nineteenth century, but they have also entered a wide variety of industrial and professional activities. Paul Laxalt, for example, United States Senator from Nevada, is descended from one of the French Basques.

As a group the Basques take pride in their heritage. Their language is Europe's oldest, although the Spanish takeover of Basque lands in 1839 caused it to become diluted with many Spanish words. The language is so complex that in this country most of the children speak English. Although the Basques married one another during the first generation, the passage of time and their involvement with other people made this arrangement difficult to continue. Nonetheless, the Basques do get together periodically as a group. Since 1928 they have held an annual Sheepherder Ball in Boise, and there is also a midsummer St. Ignatius Day picnic to honor their patron saint. Many Western universities have made an effort to preserve Basque culture. The University of Oregon has a collection of Basque songs and stories; the University of Nevada offers a course in the Basque language; and the University of Idaho collects Basque historical items.

On the East Coast the major Spanish-speaking groups, the Puerto Ricans and the Cubans, are concentrated in the New York area and southern Florida, respectively, and both made their major impact on the mainland after World War II. Aside from these points and their common language, though, the differences between the two groups overshadow their similarities.

The United States acquired Puerto Rico from Spain at the end of the Spanish-American War in 1898, and in 1917 Puerto Ricans were granted American citizenship. Puerto Ricans have been moving to the mainland throughout the twentieth century. In 1910 the census recorded 1,500 of them; by 1930 there were 53,000. Like members of other groups, those who came were escaping from a land with chronic overpopulation and insufficient employment to sustain a burgeoning population. The depression and World War II cut the flow to the mainland from the island, but beginning in 1945 the exodus soared. Relatively cheap air transportation and an abundance of unskilled and semiskilled jobs in New York City served as the magnets. As late as 1940 New York City had slightly more than 60,000 Puerto Ricans; by 1950 that figure had quadrupled. Today there are about 1.5 million Puerto Ricans scattered throughout the continental United States, with perhaps two-thirds of these in the New York area. In 1970 the other major centers for Puerto Ricans were Chicago, with a colony of about 80,000, and Philadelphia, with 27,663, but the official figures probably underestimate the actual totals. There are also Puerto Rican communities in Bridgeport, Connecticut; Rochester, New York; Dayton, Ohio; Boston, Massachusetts; Miami, Florida; Milwaukee, Wisconsin; and in numerous cities in New Jersey.

The Puerto Rican experience in New York and other major cities on the continent is probably closer to that of the European immigrants who landed on the East Coast and settled in urban areas than to that of the Mexicans or Filipinos in the West. Although there are Puerto Rican migrant workers who moved up and down the East Coast according to the seasons, essentially they are an urban people with the problems of the city's poor.

In New York they replaced the European immigrants in lower-level factory jobs—especially the Jews and Italians in the garment district—and in the city's worst slums. Like the Europeans, they spoke a foreign language but, unlike them, they encountered a color problem. Many Puerto Ricans are the products of centuries of racial mixing between the island's white and black populations. Although in Puerto Rico higher status is afforded those of lighter complexions, darker skin does not have quite the impact that it has in the United States. On the mainland, though, Puerto Ricans learned that the darker one's skin is the greater the difficulty in gaining acceptance and being able to adjust to the dominant culture. One social worker reported that, in her dealings with Puerto Rican drug addicts, inevitably the darkest member of the family was the one affected. Piri Thomas in his moving *Down These Mean Streets*, an autobiographical account of growing up in New York City's East Harlem ghetto, recalled his own difficulties in being the darkest member of his family and how bitter he felt toward his father for passing along such pigmentation to him.

To read the social and economic statistics of Puerto Ricans in New York is to recall the earlier plight of the Irish, the Jews, and the Italians. The group's annual median income of $4,969 in 1970 was lower than that of any other urban minority; its unemployment rate is double that of other segments of the population; 30 percent of all Puerto Rican families in the city live in poverty, and one out of every two families is on relief. Compared to other groups fewer Puerto Ricans graduate from high school or college, and more of their elementary-school-age children are below grade level in reading than children of other ethnic backgrounds. Puerto Ricans have a higher incidence of juvenile delinquency and more drug addicts than the dominant groups in society, and they seem more susceptible to diseases like tuberculosis and venereal disease than those who are better off financially. There are more incidents of police brutality toward them than toward the middle-class elements in society, and so forth. In a word, they are plagued with the disabilities historically associated with lower-class, poorly educated immigrants. Until American society decides to be more humane and concerned with these people, their plight will be precarious at best.

Despite these difficulties there are signs that Puerto Ricans will follow along the paths established by the European immigrants. In 1969 Joseph Montserrat, who later became the first Puerto Rican president of the New York City Board of Education, pointed out that most of the group's members were in New York for fewer than 15 years, that half of them were under 21 years of age, and that 84 percent of those of Puerto Rican ancestry born on the mainland were under 14 years old. Nevertheless, by 1960 only 25 percent of the Puerto Ricans were classified as unskilled or service workers, while the rest were rated as semiskilled, clerical and sales, craftsmen and foremen, engaged in professional, managerial, or technical occupations or working as proprietors. By 1964 Puerto Ricans owned more than 6,000 small businesses in New York City, including groceries, barber shops, and dry-cleaning stores. Since 1969 there has also been an open enrollment policy in the City University of New York, which charges no tuition, and this mandates admission to any resident high school graduate seeking entry. This policy alone will open an avenue for Puerto Ricans which was denied to members of ethnic groups in the past who were forced to fight quotas and meet standards that only a minority of the older immigrants or their children ever attained.

The major problem for the Puerto Ricans in New York City today, aside from poverty, language, and their concomitant difficulties, is that there is no visible leader of the group. Joseph Montserrat and Congressman Herman Badillo serve as models of achievement through diligence and hard work, but they are examples more of individual prowess than group accomplishment. Morever, there are no unifying organizations such as the German turnverein, the Irish Catholic Church, or the Jewish mutual-assistance societies that help members of their respective ethnic groups. The Young Lords, a militant body of teenagers, have demonstrated for free food and Puerto Rican studies programs in the colleges, and the Puerto Rican Association for Community Affairs inaugurated ASPIRA to encourage Puerto Rican youth to exploit their talents to the fullest, but they deal with relatively few people and lack the resources for mobilizing an ethnic community. The Roman Catholic Church cannot do it because the Puerto Rican attachment to Catholicism is too slight, and besides, many Puerto Ricans in New York have found the Protestant pentecostal churches more to their liking. The only institutions that have extensive contact with the Puerto Ricans are those city agencies that minister to the poor—and they are much too rigid and impersonal to provide the warmth and succor needed during the transition period in a new society.

The other Spanish-speaking minority that has made a major impact on the East Coast and the first immigrant group to change the complexion of a Southern city in the twentieth century, is the Cuban. As a group the Cubans are considerably different from every other large wave of immigrants that this country has received. First of all, the bulk of them are political refugees who left their homes because of the policies inaugurated by Castro after he led a successful revolution against the regime of Fulgencio Batista. Secondly, the Cuban refugees were among the elite of their society. According to one study, about 70 percent were professional, skilled, or white-collar workers; almost 40 percent had some college education; and 80 percent of those who came had yearly incomes above those earned by the average Cuban.

Since Miami, Florida, is the city closest to Havana in both distance and culture, most of the Cubans went there. The American government assisted them in their move from Cuba by waiving immigration requirements, providing plans for an airlift to Florida, and establishing agencies to help them in their adjustment to the United States. They have made an impressive impact in Miami since they started leaving Cuba in 1959 by moving up the economic ladder to achieve middle-class status in this country faster than any other ethnic group since the Huguenots of colonial times. By the end of 1971 the 350,000 Cubans in the Miami area made up a third of the city's population, prompting some Miami shopkeepers, only half in jest, to post signs reading "English Spoken Here." With an average family income of over $8,000 a year, more than half owned their own homes and 91 percent had automobiles. Cubans ran most of the area's best nightclubs and restaurants, controlled 30 percent of all new construction in Miami, and had 4 presidents and 36 vice-presidents of local banks. They owned one-third of the city's retail businesses, 60 percent of Miami's service stations, 20 cigar manufacturing plants, 30 furniture factories, 10 garment plants, 12 private schools, 10 phonograph-record plants, 3 radio stations, and a newspaper, *Diarios de las Americas,* with a daily circulation of 60,000. In 1962 half of the Cubans received welfare of some kind; by 1969 fewer than 10 percent required any public assistance. Unlike most other Spanish-speaking newcomers to the United States, Cuban children receiving special tutoring do exceptionally well in school. It usually takes the average Cuban child one-and-one-half years to become proficient in English and move into the regular classroom.

Because of the economic success of the Cubans and because of their anticommunism, one reads and hears mostly praise for them in the United States. They have settled in almost every part of the country in addition to southern Florida (New York City has the second largest Cuban settlement, about 80,000) and alone among urban immigrant groups of the past 150 years have avoided the decades of squalor usually associated with newcomers. As a result, they have avoided most of the bigotry and discrimination that the others have experienced. The magazine stories about the Cuban émigrés refer to them as "resourceful, aggressive, and energetic"— characteristics that most Americans have been taught to respect.

Other Spanish-speaking newcomers in the United States arrived from numerous sections of Latin America, including Colombia and the Dominican Republic, in the 1960s and 1970s and settled in the New York City area. Colombian law allows its citizens to vote in any consulate throughout the world, and in 1970 about 3,700 in the United States participated in the election. In early 1974 the major candidates in the Colombian election, fearing a close contest, organized and campaigned in the borough of Queens in New York City.

The Dominicans, forced out of their home country by desperate poverty and a 30 percent unemployment rate, also sought new opportunities in the United States. A fairly lucrative business developed in New York City and the Dominican Republic for obtaining American visas and work permits. One lawyer, half in jest, noted: "After the sugar industry hustling visas has become the biggest business there is in the Dominican Republic."

Although millions of Latin Americans now want to get into the United States, legal visas are difficult to obtain. Since 1965, in fact, when quotas were instituted for Latin Americans, the numbers of illegal entrants have increased. In 1974 the United States Department of Justice estimated that there were between 800,000 and 1 million illegal aliens in this country; others have suggested that the figure might run four or five times higher than that. Perhaps 50,000 to 100,000 from Central and South America are in New York and New Jersey. More than 90 percent of the rest, though, are probably Mexicans. César Chavez complains that wetbacks now hold about 20 percent of the 250,000 farm jobs in California and comprise the entire potato-harvesting work force in Idaho. An organizer for the International Brotherhood of Pottery and Allied Workers in Los Angeles said that these aliens are making it virtually impossible to unionize pottery and plumbing-fixture workers or to improve existing contracts. Everyone agrees that the illegal aliens work for lower wages than Americans will accept.

Mexico's population is now growing at a rate of 3.5 percent a year—one of the fastest growth rates of any nation in the world—and she cannot sustain her population. The areas on the Mexican-American border have grown especially fast since 1940. For example, Tijuana grew from 21,977 in 1940 to 347,501 in 1967 and Ciudad Juarez from 55,024 to 501,416 in the same period. Many Mexicans and other Latin Americans have been waiting eagerly for their chance to get some work and the higher wages available in the United States. Illegal aliens from Mexico and elsewhere are often exploited economically, but they do not particularly concern themselves about how they get into the United States. As one wetback admitted to a reporter in 1973, "If the police catch me, I will keep trying to come back, again and again. The life is better than any I can hope to have back home."

Although the Immigration and Naturalization Service is concerned about illegal entrants, Congress has not seen fit to provide sufficient funds for an adequate border patrol. Although agents have been funded since 1924, the patrol has been under constant pressure in the past from southwestern farm groups to relax its vigilance, especially at harvest time. The reality of the situation is that a 1,600-mile border runs between Brownsville, Texas, and San Diego, California, and only about 80 miles of this stretch is barricaded. Furthermore, only the regions around the main entry points like San Diego, Nogales (Arizona), El Paso (Texas), and a few others are well patrolled.

Complicating the problem of illegal entrants are organized smuggling rings, which are well trained to evade the authorities and bring aliens in for a fee. This crime has replaced narcotics trafficking as the key problem at the border stations. More than 1.5 million people crossed into the United States from Mexico at the border points in 1972, and a thorough checking of all entrants would have been impossible. As a result, hundreds of thousands slipped through at these stations or through some of the unguarded areas. The smugglers have been taking their charges to points in Los Angeles, Denver, Kansas City, Philadelphia, and Chicago. Recent estimates place the number of Spanish-speaking in the Chicago area as high as 300,000 to 400,000, and it is difficult to estimate how many are Puerto Ricans, how many are legal entrants from Mexico or migrants from the Southwest, and how many are illegal aliens.

Unfortunately, with the exception of the Cubans, the majority of the Spanish-speaking in this country find themselves near the bottom of the socioeconomic ladder. With so much more public assistance available than had been given to immigrants in previous generations, it is possible that the newcomers may not need as long a time to move into the mainstream of American society. On the other hand, illegal entrants are not likely to benefit from public assistance. As descendants of the European and Asian minorities discovered, however, a move into the mainstream of American life requires the relinquishment of cherished cultural ties. It remains to be seen how members of the Spanish-speaking minorities will choose to act. If the past is any guide, they will assimilate as others have before them. They know that the price they must pay for acceptance in the United States is an almost absolute conformity to the standards of the American middle class. And this is an impossibility if one holds onto the heritage of another culture.

Chapter 7

Pilgrim's Progress: Ethnic Mobility in Modern America

THE grim living conditions facing the old and new immigrants confronted their children and, sometimes, their grandchildren. Oftentimes, the newcomers moved slowly out of poverty and the ghetto, and gains witnessed by the second and third generations were sometimes lost. Yet the striking fact of immigrant history is that of social mobility, an improvement in the status and living conditions of the descendants of the millions who flocked to the United States. Progress was by no means even from group to group or from generation to generation.

Of the old immigrants the Irish probably had the most difficult time, but a few made spectacular progress and became veritable personifications of the rags-to-riches story. Robert Joseph Cuddihy began as an office boy in Funk and Wagnalls publishing house in New York City at the age of 16. Working his way up through the publishing world, he became a wealthy and powerful publisher. Joseph P. Kennedy, the son of a Boston immigrant saloon keeper and father of President John F. Kennedy, made his fortune on Wall Street and in the motion-picture business and later served as ambassador to Great Britain. John Buckley, the founder of one of America's leading conservative families, emigrated to America without much money. After a mixture of success and failure in Texas, his son, William F. Buckley, arrived in New York City nearly penniless in 1922 but soon thereafter became a millionaire. Peter McDonnell began his career as a bondsman in New York City and laid the foundation of a major Wall Street brokerage house.

But most of America's Irish moved up the social scale slowly. Working in unskilled occupations provided few opportunities for advancement. The growth of canals and railroads offered low-paying, backbreaking jobs that left the workers unemployed and practically destitute whenever and wherever the project ended. As a result, Irish settlements developed all over the country but usually at or near canal and railroad depots. The opening of mill towns in New England also created opportunities for those willing to work long and hard.

The Irish did manage to improve their lot, though, during the nineteenth century. By the 1870s in Boston they had already come to dominate the police and fire departments. Throughout the nation young Irishwomen staffed the urban elementary schools. They comprised 25 percent of the teachers in Boston and New York City in the 1880s and a generation later gained a foothold in the teaching ranks of Buffalo, Chicago and San Francisco. The most thrifty of the workers saved money to buy houses. This was possible in part because many persisted at one job and in one place year after year. The Irish also tended to marry late, thereby enabling the young workers to save enough for the down payments on modest homes. If these schemes for property accumulation proved insufficient, wives and children worked and contributed to the family coffers. Putting children to work added to the family's income, of course, but it also hurt the younger generation's chances for future mobility.

Accomplishments in many businesses, though, were achieved at a time when education was not as necessary as it would later become. The construction industry, for example, boomed along with the growth of urban America. The Irish, using the influence of friends in city hall, became contractors and builders. By 1890 there were two times as many of them in these occupations as other immigrant groups. In Philadelphia Edward J. Lafferty constructed the city's waterworks, and James P. "Sunny Jim" McNichol, another Irish politician-contractor, helped build the city's subways, sewers, and water-filtration plant.

During the twentieth century, and especially after World War II, the Irish progressed rapidly to middle and upper middle-class status. They ran businesses, worked in banks and insurance companies, and became doctors, lawyers, professors, civil servants, and technicians. The occupational distribution of the American Irish in the 1970s resembled that of the northern urban Anglo-Saxon Protestants. Among the white Catholics in America, the Irish usually had more education, better jobs, and higher incomes. Few could claim the fabulous wealth of America's most famous Irish family, the Kennedys, but not many were poor, either. The American Irish had at long last arrived.

To consider the Irish experience solely in terms of the move from shanties to suburban homes and from ditch diggers to lawyers gives an incomplete picture. In two special vocational areas —the Roman Catholic Church and politics—the Irish had experiences that were unique, not because they were so lucrative but because the ethnic group valued these positions. To have a son become a lawyer or doctor was, of course, a sign of success, but the Irish also considered it important to give a son and a daughter to the Church.

That the Irish dominated the Catholic Church in America is not surprising. In Ireland the Church was the carrier of the faith and a source of comfort in the face of English oppression. It served a similar function in America. The hostility of native Protestant Americans to the Irish and Catholicism only made the Church more important, for it provided a bulwark of security to the embattled Irish immigrant.

Shortly after the Irish arrived in the 1840s, they became the dominant group in the American Catholic hierarchy. From Archbishop John Hughes of New York to Baltimore's James Cardinal Gibbons, the first American cardinal, and on to New York's Francis Cardinal Spellman, the leading American Catholics have usually been of Irish origin. They supported the parochial schools, sent their sons and daughters to do God's work, and gave what they could from their meager incomes for religious activities. When large numbers of non-Irish Catholics, such as the Italians, arrived in America, they often resented Irish control of the Church and demanded their own clergy and parishes. The Church disapproved of nationality or ethnic parishes in principle, but, nonetheless, the practice existed among the Germans, Poles, and French Canadians. In the twentieth century Irish control of the Church hierarchy gradually lessened, but it never disappeared. In the early 1970s the Irish constituted fewer than one-fifth of the Catholics in the United States but about one-third of the clergy and one-half of the hierarchy.

Irish domination of urban politics was not so complete as that of the Church, but it was impressive. New York City elected a Roman Catholic mayor in 1880, and Boston followed suit four years later. Before the end of the century Irish "bosses" dominated local politics in New York, Jersey City, Hoboken, Boston, Chicago, Buffalo, Albany and Troy (New York), Pittsburgh, St. Paul, St. Louis, Kansas City (Missouri), Omaha, New Orleans, and San Francisco. New York City's famed Tammany Hall passed into Irish hands when "Honest John" (his enemies called him crooked as a ram's horn) Kelly succeeded Protestant boss William M. Tweed in 1874, and it remained under Irish control for the next 80 years. Bosses Frank Hague of Jersey City and Tom Pendergast of Kansas City, Missouri, were legends in their day, as is Mayor Richard Daley of Chicago in his.

None of the Irish urban politicians was so extraordinary as James Michael Curley of Boston. He served in local offices before becoming U.S. congressman, mayor of the city, and then governor of Massachusetts. Curley symbolized many aspects of the Irish style in politics. He maintained his contacts with the Church and the Irish community and was a skillful showman. He played upon the Irish resentment of Boston's Yankees and Brahmins to build a personal following, and he provided jobs and social services for the poor. He also knew how to appeal to his followers: "My mother was obliged to work ... as a scrubwoman toiling nights in office buildings downtown. I thought of her one night while leaving City Hall during my first term as Mayor. I told the scrubwomen cleaning the corridors to get up; 'The only time a woman should go down on her knees is when she is praying to Almighty God,' I said. Next morning I ordered longhandled mops and issued an order that scrubwomen were never again to get down on their knees in City Hall." Critics attacked Curley for corruption, but no matter—he still won elections even while in jail.

The Irish reach for the presidency occurred in 1928 when Al Smith from the Lower East Side of New York City became a candidate. He rose quickly through New York City's Democratic organization (that is, Tammany Hall) and served as state legislator and governor before grasping for the big prize. Smith epitomized the Irish Catholic politician, a factor that worked both for and against him in 1928. He opposed prohibition, attacked the immigration restriction laws, and was a devout Catholic. As a result, he won the

Catholic and immigrant vote in many places and reversed Democratic fortunes of the 1920s by capturing a dozen or so of the nation's largest cities. The Democratic presidential candidate amassed more popular votes than any of his predecessors ever had. (Part of the explanation for this, no doubt, was that a larger percentage of women voted in 1928 than had in 1920 or 1924.) Nevertheless, many Protestants feared that the Roman Catholic Church would exert a strong influence on a Catholic in the White House and voted Republican for the first time in their lives.

After Smith's defeat no Irish Catholic and no other member of an ethnic minority group made the bid for the presidency until John F. Kennedy's triumph in 1960. Keenly aware that politicos still regarded his Roman Catholic faith as a severe handicap, Kennedy faced the religious issue squarely. His primary victory in West Virginia proved he could win Protestant votes, and his smooth political machine achieved a first-ballot victory at the Democratic convention. Yet the religious issue would not die, and Kennedy had to make several strong statements about his belief in the separation of church and state. In the election Kennedy lost some votes because of his Catholicism, but he ran strongly in the heavily Catholic Northeast and slipped into the presidency by the narrowest margin of any victorious candidate since Woodrow Wilson in 1916.

Kennedy's election, culminating a century of Irish political activity, was built upon the previous victories of Irish politicians in city wards. His religious commitments were public knowledge as were his ties to the Irish community. Some even said an "Irish Mafia" had won him the nomination. A few Catholics went to the other extreme and insisted that Kennedy was not Catholic enough. Kennedy was clearly different from both Al Smith and James Curley. Born into a wealthy family, educated at Choate and Harvard, he was highly assimilated, cosmopolitan, and intellectual, and he did not seem particularly Irish—except for political purposes. Whether another type of Irish politician could have won in 1960 is debatable, but the old ward boss was a thing of the past by then. The Irish had arrived in politics as they had in business and the Church.

The largest of the old immigrant groups, the Germans, generally rose faster than the Irish. They had certain advantages over the Irish, namely, that they were not so poor when they arrived and often had more education. Many Germans, unlike the Irish, farmed successfully, but most lived in or later moved to the cities. Those without skills or education took laboring jobs, but many became skilled workers in America's growing industries. They were also cabinetmakers, bakers, tailors, bookbinders, and furniture makers, and they often were the leaders in the craft unions. For example, the bakers' unions in the 1870s and 1880s were solidly German. Some of the German workers even veered off into radical politics.

German immigrants and their children did well in business and were an established minority by the time of World War I. They brought with them their love of beer drinking and beer-making skills, and they founded breweries that became virtually a German monopoly in the early twentieth century. St. Louis and Milwaukee are centers of the beer business, and names like Pabst, Miller, Schlitz, Schaefer, and Anheuser-Busch became household words in twentieth-century America. They also ran beer gardens, hotels and restaurants like Mader's in Milwaukee and Luchow's in New York City. One observer commented about the beer gardens: "The commencement of one of these establishments appears to be very simple. A German obtains a cellar, a cask of beer, a cheese, a loaf of bread, and some pretzels—puts out a sign and the business is started." Although the breweries and beer gardens were the most notable German connections to the liquor business, a few Germans, such as Paul Krug, developed vineyards in California.

Germans also excelled in other areas of American business enterprise. George Westinghouse, a poor farm boy from upstate New York, patented the air brake for trains and then founded a major corporation. Another inventor businessman, Charles Steinmetz, became known as the wizard of Schenectady and was the dynamic force behind the huge General Electric Company. Although Steinmetz had a European education, he arrived at Ellis Island from Germany without funds and a job. Indeed, he was almost deported. His mastery of electricity led him to fame and fortune. John A. Roebling, another innovator, put his ideas about steel cables to use in building suspension bridges. Roebling died while supervising the construction of his most famous bridge, the Brooklyn Bridge.

Other Germans used their talents in the ethnic community as clergymen and editors of German periodicals and newspapers, which were numerous on the eve of World War I, or operated small businesses that catered to the German-American community. A few branched out into politics like Robert Wagner of New York or the socialist Victor Berger of Milwaukee. These politicians, like the Irish, built their strength on the ethnic vote and through service to the ethnic communities. Earlier, Germans had elected congressmen and senators regularly after the Civil War and governors in Illinois and Kentucky in the 1890s.

Germans also excelled in music. City orchestras in the nineteenth century were heavily German, and German singers were popular in America, as were German singing societies. Besides playing musical instruments, Germans also made them. Steinway and Sons was the most famous of the German piano makers, but others, such as Knabe, Weber, and Wurlitzer, were well known too.

Although World War I was a shattering experience for many German Americans and caused many of their institutions in America to decline, it did not impede their socioeconomic progress. They prospered in practically every key area of American business, in the professions—as doctors, lawyers, and engineers, in government and science. They were well represented among the American corporate elite, had high educational levels and solid incomes. Not many were poor. So much were the descendants of German immigrants a part of American life that few Americans conceived of them as a distinct ethnic group. Nevertheless President Richard Nixon's chief White House assistants from 1969 to 1973, H. R. Haldeman and John Ehrlichman, were known to a number of Washingtonians as the "German shepherds."

Like the Germans, the Swedes have also prospered. The children and grandchildren of many of those who tilled the soil in the Upper Midwest sought their opportunities in burgeoning cities like Minneapolis and Chicago. In the urban areas they became skilled workers and clerks and gradually moved into better jobs. As a group the Swedes prospered about as well as the Germans; in the twentieth century they were second only to the British in their proportion of skilled workers in America. A few even advanced into the business elite; Swedish-born Rudolph A. Peterson, for example, became president of the giant Bank of America in 1961. A minority remained farmers and prospered on the land.

The Norwegians were similar to the Swedes in their immigration patterns, migrating into the Upper Midwest to become farmers and farm laborers. But the Norwegians were also sailors and found jobs as seamen in American ports; they were especially important on the

West Coast. Like the Swedes, Norwegians became increasingly urbanized after 1900, and many came to America with skills that they
could use in the expanding industrial society. By the 1970s Norwegian Americans had done well and had generally moved into the
middle class, with many becoming successful businessmen, skilled
workers, and professionals. Of course, politics was open in areas
where the Norwegians and Swedes were numerous. In 1892 Knute
Nelson, with the aid of his fellow Norwegians, won the governorship of Minnesota, and Swedish and Norwegian names have been
prominent in the politics of Minnesota, Wisconsin, and the ad-
jacent states since then.

The Finns in America were slower to move up the occupational
ladder compared to their Swedish and Norwegian neighbors. Of
the Protestant groups immigrating after 1880 the Finns were the
least skilled, and this no doubt accounts for some of their difficulties
in achieving occupational mobility. Like other Scandinavians they
generally settled in the Midwest but were less apt to become farmers.
They moved frequently in search of work and were especially numerous in the mining regions of the Upper Midwest. They often
worked in company towns, where opportunities for mobility were
not abundant for those beginning without skills. Finns also tried
to found their own businesses but were not notably successful. Thus
they were more like the new immigrants than the old. Later generations did finally move out of the unskilled ranks and compete
more successfully, but they usually lagged behind the Swedes and
Norwegians.

None of the old immigrants, not even the Irish, were so scorned
as the Chinese. After the Chinese had been forced out of mines and
had helped build the railroads and raise crops in California, they
drifted to the cities in search of employment. A few were successful merchants, but most found urban life harsh and jobs limited.
They worked as domestics, as cigar makers or in other low-paying
industries. Most important to the livelihood of Chinese Americans was the laundry. The proverbial Chinese laundry developed
largely because they could find little else to do. The shortage of
women on the frontier left the laundry, a domestic service considered woman's work, open to the Chinese. A laundry required
little skill and practically no capital, only soap, a scrubboard, an
iron, an ironing board, and long hours of hard labor. Laundries
were usually one-man or family enterprises. As the Chinese moved

into the cities or to the East, they took their laundries with them. By 1880 over 7,000 Chinese made their living in laundries in San Francisco alone, and in 1920 the U.S. Census Bureau reported that nearly a third of employed Chinese were engaged in laundry work.

In addition to the laundries, restaurants and groceries were important to the Chinese community. Chinese restaurants originated in the mining camps along the railroads, where the Chinese prepared their own food. They preferred their own food, and the bosses agreed that it was cheaper than furnishing an American diet. The Chinese discovered that others liked their cuisine too; chop suey and chow mein, two staples of Chinese restaurants, originated in America. Restaurants required some capital, hence they were not as numerous as laundries. But like the laundries, they were often family businesses and served as an outlet for entrepreneurs blocked from other jobs.

Groceries were the third main small business of the Chinese but were not so important as the restaurants and laundries. Nevertheless, enterprising businessmen found outlets for their skills and energies. In the South and West, Chinese groceries thrived, and a few later expanded into supermarkets.

Until World War II the Chinese-American community had many service workers, small proprietors and operatives, and few professional and technical workers. But a strong family system, a commitment to education, and hard work, led to changing patterns after 1945. Declining prejudice, especially during World War II when America was an ally of China, also helped. The Chinese-American community of the 1970s was different from that of a century before. By 1960 many Chinese had moved into the middle class. Opportunities in laundries and other undesirable forms of employment were shunned, while larger numbers engaged in technical and professional work. Particularly in mathematics and science the Chinese made a name for themselves; several, such as Chen Ning Yang and Yzyng Dao Lee, won Nobel prizes. Veneration for learning and scholarship was revealed by the fact that in the 1960s proportionately more Chinese than Caucasians had completed college.

In business, while the laundries were declining, restaurants still thrived, and the Chinese found new opportunities in finance and trade. With a small population to build a political base upon, politics was not a common way up the social ladder; but in Hawaii, with its large Chinese population, it was more possible. Hiram Fong made his political career there. He began as Deputy Attorney for the city and county of Honolulu, then moved into the legislature and finally ended up in the United States Senate.

Fong's career in some ways symbolizes the rise of Chinese Americans. Born into a large and poor family, he began work as a farm laborer. But he was an enterprising young man and worked his way through the University of Hawaii and Harvard Law School. He became a successful lawyer and businessman before he launched his political career. Since World War II other Chinese Americans have won elective offices.

As successful as Chinese Americans were after World War II, the picture was not uniformly bright. Some were still poor and jammed into overcrowded Chinatowns. Many were aged members of the old bachelor society or families that had not shared in the advantages of the younger generation. Still others were recent immigrants who had come when the quotas were loosened after 1965. As we have noted, some of these immigrants made low wages as waiters or in sweatshops reminiscent of the old immigrant neighborhoods. Thus the Chinese pattern of success was spotty.

Of the millions of immigrants coming after 1880, the so-called new immigrants, no group experienced such startling success as the Jews. Sephardic Jews, who came in the colonial period, were already solidly middle class by the time the German Jews arrived before the Civil War. Many German Jews had been traders in Germany, and they took up peddling and storekeeping in the New World. Spreading out over the nation, they made rapid progress in commerce and trade. The Lehmans and Seligmans achieved prominence in finance and banking, while Benjamin Altman and Adam Gimbel became major department-store owners. A study made in 1889 of 18,000 gainfully employed Jews, most of whom were from German-speaking countries, found that approximately one-third were retailers; 15 percent were bankers; 17 percent accountants, bookkeepers, clerks, and copyists; and 12 percent were salesmen, commercial travelers, and agents.

The bulk of the Eastern European Jews, coming after 1880, were poor but they too succeeded in America in the twentieth century. By the 1970s family incomes of America's Jews were higher than those of any other ethnic group, including the elite white Protestant Episcopalians. And their educational level was also high.

Almost 90 percent of the Jews of college age were attending institutions of higher education in the 1970s, and a high proportion were in graduate and professional schools.

Of the first generation from eastern Europe, a majority worked in the garment industry and in trade, with only a few in the professions. Jews were involved in the formation—and in their early years made up most of the members—of both the ILGWU and the Amalgamated Clothing Workers Union, founded in 1910 and 1914, respectively. The children of these union members more often than not acquired college educations and sought higher-status occupations. Anti-Semitism in the professions, including discriminatory quotas in medical schools, made it harder to achieve professional mobility, but it was accomplished nonetheless. Statistics of the late 1960s indicated that about half of all gainfully employed adult Jews engaged in a professional activity, more than double the figure for Protestants and Catholics. And in the early 1970s yearly incomes for a majority of Jewish families, whose head was typically between 30 and 59 years of age, averaged over $16,-000, compared to a national average for all families of under $11,000.

Second-generation Jews usually chose professions in which they could be independently employed and not subject to the bigotry of prejudiced employers. As a result many became physicians, lawyers, accountants, pharmacists, and dentists. In the 1930s and even in the 1960s, Jews made up more than half of New York City's dentists, physicians, and lawyers. The third generation of Jews still found law and medicine attractive, but the decline of discriminatory hiring practices opened up new opportunities for them in the academic and corporate worlds. Henry Kissinger and Irving S. Shapiro (mentioned earlier as the newly appointed chief executive of DuPont) are perhaps the outstanding examples of how far Jews have been able to rise when the sole criteria have been performance and potential.

Although individual Jews can be found in almost every line of business and professional endeavor, as a group the East Europeans have made their greatest impact in the clothing, entertainment, and intellectual worlds of American society. By the earliest years of the twentieth century the manufacture of ready-to-wear clothing was in the hands of Jewish owners. In 1950 more than 85 percent of American-made clothes were manufactured in Jewish-owned shops. In the entertainment field both the theatre and the movies provided avenues of mobility for Jewish actors, actresses, writers, tunesmiths, directors, and producers. Two Russian-born Jews, David Sarnoff and William Paley, developed what one financial publication called "perhaps the world's two greatest broadcasting empires," the Radio Corporation of America (RCA) and the Columbia Broadcasting System (CBS), respectively. In the intellectual community leading journals such as *Commentary,* since 1945, and *The New York Review of Books,* for the past decade or so, have relied on Jewish sponsors and/or editors. Authors like Norman Mailer, Philip Roth, Saul Bellow, Bernard Malamud, and Meyer Levin have been among the major figures in American literature in the past three decades. And in academia prominent scholars like historian Oscar Handlin, social scientist Seymour Martin Lipset, and economist Simon Kuznets are a credit to the faculties of the nation's leading universities. Artist Ben Shahn, the discoverer of the polio vaccine, Jonas Salk, film maker Stanley Kubrick, violinist Yehudi Menuhin, musician Leonard Bernstein, and former Supreme Court Justice and Ambassador to the United Nations Arthur Goldberg—these are only a few of the Jews of East European descent who have distinguished themselves in American society. Not all Jews, of course, are as prominent and accomplished as the aforementioned group, but it is worth noting that no twentieth-century minority has risen as fast, in terms of social and economic mobility, as the descendants of those Jews who arrived from eastern Europe at the turn of the century.

The remarkable success of Jews was undoubtedly the product of hard work, skill, and an arduous struggle in an expanding economy. Their traditional respect for learning facilitated advancement because education was an important vehicle for social mobility. To what extent American public schools really served the immigrants is a subject of debate and in need of study, but in the case of Jewish immigrants they were of great advantage. Parents pushed their children to achieve, and they themselves, eager for an education, attended the public evening schools. As journalist Abraham Cahan, chronicler of the Lower East Side of New York City, put it, "The ghetto rang with a clamor for knowledge."

In addition to their respect for education, Jews brought with them an urban living experience and skills that could be used in commercial and industrial America. Though Jews faced tensions and problems common to all immigrant groups, their families were relatively stable, providing a sense of security as well as a springboard for their children. The older German-Jewish community, another extraordinarily accomplished group, with its many welfare agencies, was sometimes suspicious of and hostile to the greenhorns from eastern Europe with their different dress, language, and ideas; but on the whole it was a source of strength to the newcomers. Inadvertently, anti-Semitism united and strengthened the entire Jewish community and prompted many of the more successful to help their less fortunate kin.

Also to be reckoned with are the intangibles, such as the culture of the immigrant group, which cannot be precisely measured. Certainly, there was a clash between Protestantism and Judaism, but in many ways there was an agreement over key values. Jews found it easier than did some others to accept the American stress upon achievement and mobility. The differences over religion did not lead to the rejection of these broader American values, but, on the contrary, more than one analyst has observed how readily Jewish Americans accepted the Protestant ethic of hard work and material accomplishment.

Perhaps the reasons for Jewish emigration also had something to do with their success in the United States. They came, like so many others, to find a better life, but, unlike many others, they could not return to the Old World. The pogroms that had driven them away dimmed most hopes for returning. Because they had to make it here—not in the Old World—Jews came with a determination to make America truly the Promised Land.

As we have seen the Italians had a somewhat different experience. They were probably poorer than the Jews and coming from a rural background, were unfamiliar with city life. A large number were only interested in collecting a bit of cash in order to return to Italy. For many Italians success meant returning home with something, not achieving status in the United States. Often they moved from job to job and finally back to Italy. Consequently, they did not experience the rapid social mobility that Jews did, but they gradually prospered nonetheless.

Although most Italians lived in cities, a few succeeded on the land. On both the East and West coasts Italians became skillful truck farmers and supplied the growing urban areas with food. The di Giorgio orchards eventually covered 40,000 acres in California.

More famous were the wineries of California like Italian-Swiss Colony and Gallo Brothers. In 1971 the Gallo Winery had revenues of a quarter of a billion dollars. Along with German wines, Italian-American wines became the best known in American stores. A few Italians also became successful in the South raising cotton, sugar cane, and other crops.

Like all other ethnic groups, the Italian have their notable success stories. Among northern Italians the career of Amadeo P. Giannini, founder of the Bank of America, is outstanding. Giannini began as a banker for immigrants but expanded his operations in the early twentieth century. When the San Francisco earthquake struck in 1906, he rescued his bank's gold, hidden in a produce wagon, and was quickly ready to open business again. Expanding from San Francisco's North Beach Italian colony, he branched out and became a major factor in the state's growing economy. He saw the future in branch banking and expanded from real estate to industrial financing. When he retired in 1945, the Bank of America had become the largest private bank in the world, with $5.5 billion in deposits and over 3 million depositors.

Other Italians became successful and sometimes wealthy in business. Some were importers of products such as olive oil, macaroni, and ravioli, while others were producers of ethnic goods in demand by Italian Americans and later other Americans as well. They also ran groceries and opened restaurants.

For most, however, success came gradually and not spectacularly. Beginning as garment workers in New York City, day laborers or miners in Pennsylvania, or in other unskilled or semiskilled jobs, Italian Americans found the path upward difficult. Although some individuals made giant leaps, the second generation improved itself over the first modestly, becoming construction workers and foremen, small businessmen, and lesser white-collar workers rather than unskilled laborers, factory workers, and miners. After World War II the third generation made greater progress. As job opportunities expanded due to the decline of prejudice, some Italian Americans even found new chances in large businesses, finance, and the professions. In the early 1970s the presidents of the Ford Motor Company and the Chrysler Corporation, for example, were Lee A. Iococca and John Riccardo, both of Italian descent. In part, too, the Italian-American community was beginning to recognize the economic advantages of higher education. Until after World War

II most of those who attended college were of northern Italian descent, but this trend began to change after the war. Even so, the general educational level of Italian Americans was less than the American average for whites. In the 1960s, for instance, less than 5 percent of native-born Italian Americans were completing college, a figure below the national average. For those having education, prestige jobs were opening and with them the possibility of higher incomes. In general, Italian Americans were achieving a middle-class status, not the equal of Jews or even the Irish, but ahead of recent immigrant groups like Mexican Americans and Puerto Ricans.

Settling in large numbers in urban areas and being Catholic opened other possibilities to Italians for broader participation and achievement, in particular with regard to the Catholic Church and in politics. However, the Irish controlled the Church and played a large role in determining urban politics. Not until after World War II did Italian Americans begin to break into the hierarchy of American Catholicism. In 1967 the grandson of an Italian immigrant became bishop of the diocese embracing Mississippi, and a year later another Italian American became bishop of Brooklyn, the largest diocese in the United States. Although Italians were moving up in the church by the 1970s, they were still underrepresented in the hierarchy.

Once Italians began to register and vote in American elections, they began to rise politically. But in this case too the move upward was slow. Before World War II the most successful Italian-American politician was congressman and later mayor of New York, Fiorello La Guardia. La Guardia was somewhat of an anomaly. He was Protestant, not Catholic; he had a Jewish mother, and he could speak several languages. He also tried to appeal to many groups, not only Italian Americans. San Francisco with its large Italian population also had an Italian mayor in the 1930s, but not until after the war did Italian Americans make many breakthroughs politically. In 1946 in Rhode Island John O. Pastore became the first man of Italian background to be elected governor of a state. Rhode Island later sent Pastore to the United States Senate, the first Italian American elected to the upper house of Congress. Increasingly, in the 1950s and 1960s Italians were elected to important political offices as congressmen, state legislators, and mayors of big cities. Perhaps symbolic of the political arrival of Italian Americans was Carmine G. De Sapio's takeover of the leadership of New York's Tammany Hall in 1949. Irish hegemony was clearly on the wane in big cities, and Italians were one of the groups benefitting from it. By 1974 two men of Italian descent, Meade H. Esposito, a Brooklyn Democrat, and Assemblyman Joseph M. Margiotta, a Nassau County Republican, were regarded as two of the most powerful political bosses in New York State. Esposito headed a typically urban enclave of mixed ethnic groups, while Margiotta, who symbolizes what *The New York Times* called "the coming of age, politically, of the suburbs," controlled "the most effective political machine east of Chicago." He presided over a prosperous and predominantly white, Americanized homogeneous group more akin to the white, Anglo-Saxon Protestant (WASP) critics of urban bossism of yesteryear than to the greenhorns of another era, who depended on their local politicians to ease the adjustment to the New World. Esposito ran his domain, like the bosses of old, "as a series of fiefdoms to be placated, appeased and sometimes bossed." Margiotta, on the other hand, handled his organization "like the $1 million corporation it is."

Italians have also won attention for their participation in organized criminal activities. In the 1950s Senator Estes Kefauver of Tennessee conducted hearings about crime in America and paraded Italian-American gangsters before the committee and a national television audience. Kefauver said that the Mafia was controlled by Italian Americans and Italians in Italy, and it was "the shadowy international organization that lurks behind much of organized criminal activity." The charge that Italians in America were involved with the Mafia was not new. As early as 1891 the New York *Tribune* had insisted that "in large cities throughout the country, Italians of criminal antecedents and propensities are more or less closely affiliated for the purpose of requiting injuries and gratifying animosities by secret vengeances. These organizations in common speech and belief are connected with the *Mafia,* and that designation fairly indicates their character and motives. Through their agency the most infernal crimes have been committed and have gone unpunished."

Certainly some Italian Americans have been involved in organized crime. As Humbert Nelli, historian of Italians in Chicago, put it:

Crime, one means of economic advancement independent of education, social background or political connections, provided for all
classes of Italians opportunities for quick and substantial monetary
gain and sometimes for social and political advancement as well.
Within the colony bankers and padroni, blackhanders and other law-
breakers all realized small but important profits by swindling or ter-
rorizing compatriots. The "syndicate," a business operation reaping
vast profits from the American community, offered almost limitless
opportunities for promotion within its hierarchy. Thus for some,
crime offered means of advancement within the ethnic community
and for others, opportunities outside it.

How many or what percentage of Italians and their children engaged in such work is impossible to determine. Popular accounts
and later stereotypes about the Black Hand, the Mafia, and members of *Cosa Nostra* emphasized unduly this type of endeavor among
Italians and Italian Americans.

Al Capone, the Italian-American leader of crime in Chicago
during the violent and colorful days of prohibition in the 1920s,
was the prototype of the big-city gangster. Others followed Capone
to prominence after his demise in the 1930s. A few were convicted,
and when evidence of criminal acts was lacking, the United States
government deported as undesirable aliens some of those born in
Italy.

Italian Americans, though, have not monopolized organized
crime. Historians and sociologists remind us that various other
ethnic groups have been associated with criminal activity. In the
nineteenth century the Irish were notorious as criminals in New
York City's Five Points District, and crime has always been a part
of ghetto life in this country; as the ethnic occupants of the slums
change, so do the names on the police arrest lists. One study of
the top underworld figures in Chicago in 1930 estimated that 30
percent were of Italian background, 29 percent of Irish background,
and 20 percent of Jewish background. While Capone was famous
in the Chicago rackets of the 1920s, Dean O'Banion, and men
like Arnold Rothstein and Meyer Lansky were prominent in New
York City.

It should also be kept in mind the extent to which criminal
activities were an avenue of social mobility. Old-stock Americans
dominated the powerful positions in American industry, banking,

insurance, and commerce. With few exceptions they have always been loath to allow the immigrants or their children opportunities for advancement to the middle and upper levels of management. Crime, accordingly, was a way out of the ghetto and a means of achieving material success. Reluctantly, some chose it, though for others the choice was not always reluctant.

Another point that must be made is that while certain activities are legally considered crimes, not everyone in the country makes the same assessment. Some ethnic groups did not share the old-stock white Protestant aversion to gambling and drinking. Swedes and some pietistic Protestant immigrants did, perhaps, but others did not think it so terribly wrong to gamble or to supply liquor to thirsty throats during Prohibition. Besides, it was the so-called respectable citizens' patronage of illegal liquor that made Prohibition a failure. President Warren G. Harding drank during his tenure in the White House, and it was rumored that he and his cronies supported private bootleggers. As Al Capone asked: "What's Al Capone done, then? He supplied a legitimate demand. Some call it bootlegging. Some call it racketeering. I call it a business. They say I violate the prohibition law. Who doesn't?"

If crime has been a path upward for older immigrants, there is evidence that more recent migrants to the city will follow a similar pattern as others move into the more respectable occupations. One scholar recently suggested that his research indicated that blacks, Puerto Ricans, and Cubans were already moving to take over organized crime as other minorities had done before them. Or as one Italian American said, "I guess it's their turn now."

Even though only a few Italian Americans have been associated with crime, it has left an impression that many have difficulty forgetting. The revelations of the Kefauver committee and best-selling books like *The Godfather* have produced a sense of shame and indignation at the stereotype of the Italian criminal. In 1972 Frank Sinatra complained in *The New York Times* that "there is a form of bigotry abroad in this land which allows otherwise decent people . . . to believe the most scurrilous tales if they are connected to an Italian-American name."

The experiences and paths of mobility of the other ethnic groups that were part of the great surge from southern and eastern Europe at the end of the nineteenth and beginning of the twentieth centuries vary from those of the Italians and to a considerable extent from one another. The Greeks were apt to be entrepreneurs, for example, restaurateurs, theatre owners, and food processors, or else they became professionals, such as doctors, lawyers, and teachers. The career of Alexander Pantages was similar to that of other wealthy ethnic minorities. He came from a middle-class background but made his fortune in the entertainment world. After emigrating to the United States and working at odd jobs, he made money in gold in the Yukon country and then made a fortune in the movie-house business, owning at one time a chain of 80 theatres. The Skouras brothers also owned a large number of movie houses, and Spyros Skouras became president of a major Hollywood organization, Twentieth-Century-Fox. Although the careers of Pantages and the Skourases were exceptional, most Greek Americans were ensconced in the middle class by the 1970s.

The Slavic peoples also began largely as unskilled workers in industrial America, but the second and third generations did not improve their positions as fast as some others of European descent. The working-class districts of American cities were often centers of Polish, Hungarian, and Russian life. These were areas of neat and well-kept houses, not prosperous but substantial. Like the Irish before them, they prized home ownership and invested their savings in their homes and neighborhoods. Disproportionately members of the working class, their offspring were mainly trade unionists and blue-collar workers. A survey of Slavs in Connecticut in the 1960s showed, for example, that 40 percent belonged to unions. Slavic Americans generally had incomes lower than those of the Irish or Jews or white Protestants, and their educational levels were also low. They had often found the schools, which are important for mobility, inhospitable, and many dropped out before completing high school.

Although just reaching the middle-class income level by the 1970s, many Slavs were continuing their education, moving up the economic ladder and becoming prominent in American political life as well. In the early 1930s Anton Cermak became the first Czech mayor of Chicago, but most breakthroughs occurred later. Like most other immigrants they were slow to become involved in politics, but the second and third generations began to assert themselves more effectively. In 1958 the Polish-American press claimed that 13 Americans of Polish background had been elected to Congress, and Poles were important politically in cities like Chicago, Cleveland, Milwaukee, and Buffalo. In 1968 Edmund Muskie of Maine became the first American of Polish extraction to run for vice-president, the same year that Spiro Agnew, the first politically prominent Greek American, ran for that office.

Of the new immigrants no group experienced the shock the Japanese Americans suffered during World War II. Those interned on the West Coast lost nearly everything they had, including their stake in agriculture and small businesses. Beginning from scratch after World War II, they rapidly improved their position. The key to much of the Japanese-American success was education. After 1940 the Japanese had a higher educational level than whites, with a high proportion going to college. In the 1960s and early 1970s nearly 90 percent of third-generation Japanese Americans were attending some college or university. Their attainments combined with lessening prejudice led to better jobs and higher incomes.

In Hawaii the Japanese were not interned, but their status was not especially high on the eve of World War II. Once again, after the war the second and third generations on the islands made rapid strides, with many becoming engineers, physicians, and lawyers. Even political life beckoned after the war. The Issei, the first generation, was ineligible for citizenship and hence excluded from politics. But members of the native-born second generation were automatically citizens, and in Hawaii their numbers made them a potential political force. Sharp increases in the number of registered voters on the islands were translated into electoral victories. In 1968 both members of the House of Representatives from Hawaii and its Democratic United States senator, Daniel Inouye, were of Japanese ancestry. Japanese Americans were also well represented in state and local offices of Hawaii.

Leaving individual ethnic groups, we now turn to an area in which the children and grandchildren of immigrants participated on an equal footing—the world of athletics. In this realm above all others individual skill rather than one's ethnic background determined success. And once successful, doors to social and economic mobility opened wide. (Athletics, in fact, might be compared to entertainment as one of the great levelers in American society except that until after World War II blacks were restricted from most areas of competition.) Sports, therefore, has been a way many members of ethnic groups escaped working-class lives. Many of the famed nineteenth-century boxers like John L. Sullivan and James Corbett were Irish, and Notre Dame's great football team of the 1930s, coached by Knute Rockne, was known as "the fighting Irish." Gertrude Ederle, the first woman to swim the English Channel, was of German descent. In baseball other Germans found fame and sometimes fortune. Lou Gehrig, Honus Wagner, Rube Wadell, and the greatest German-American player of all, Babe Ruth, born George Herman Erhardt in Baltimore, were idols in their day. The DiMaggio brothers were the most famous of the Italian baseball players, while Stan Musial, Ed Lopat, and Ted Kluszewski were of Polish ancestry. In our own day blacks and Spanish-speaking Americans are finding the world of professional athletics one arena in which they can compete and are judged strictly on the basis of their talents and individual accomplishments.

Obviously, most of the descendants of immigrants could not be outstanding athletes and had to take the more usual paths—white-collar and professional positions—to middle-class security. Better jobs provided higher incomes and led them out of the ghettos. At first the move was to better neighborhoods in the city, but since the end of World War II the trek has been increasingly to the suburbs. In New York City in the late 1920s fewer than 10 percent of the Jews still lived on the famed Lower East Side. The completion of the subways stimulated the exodus to the upper reaches of Manhattan and the Bronx and across the East River into Brooklyn. In Chicago the original Italian districts declined in the 1920s. The subsequent depression and the post–World War II housing shortage curtailed movement, but the affluence of the 1950s rejuvenated it. The growth of suburbia in the 1950s and 1960s can be attributed to a great extent to the movement of the children and grandchildren of the Irish, Italians, Poles, Jews, and Scandinavians who had shared in the nation's growing prosperity. So great was the move that by 1970 the census showed more people who were overwhelmingly white living in suburban America than in the central cities.

In many cases the pattern of movement went far beyond the neighboring green belts. Sunshine and job opportunities drew people to the South and the West. Florida and California in particular more than doubled their populations in the decades since the end of World War II, and the growth in job opportunities in regional centers such as Washington, D.C., and Dallas, Texas, also resulted in mushrooming populations.

Although the suburban growth drew many away from the cities, the old ethnic neighborhoods, the little Italies, Polands, Tokyos, and the like did not disappear completely. The Slavs and Italians, less affluent and strongly attached to their homes and old family neighborhoods, were the last to leave, and many simply remained where they were. As a result there are still ethnic enclaves of Italians in New York City and Newark, New Jersey, and Slavic neighborhoods in Philadelphia, Detroit, Milwaukee, Cleveland, Pittsburgh, and Buffalo. Moreover, refugee arrivals since 1945 strengthened some of the old ethnic neighborhoods. Just as the descendants of the original Chinese were moving out of the Chinatowns in America, renewed immigration in the 1960s and 1970s once again swelled their population. Similarly, refugee Hasidic Jews reinforced the Jewish population of Brooklyn when they settled in the Williamsburg, Crown Heights, and Borough Park sections.

Yet the general trend was clear. The older and more prosperous immigrants' descendants measured their success by their movement, leaving behind the less affluent and the more recent arrivals, the blacks, Mexican Americans, Cubans, Puerto Ricans, and other Latin Americans. This was particularly noticeable in the major metropolises. In New York City, the symbol of the nation's ethnic diversity and the port of entry for so many newcomers, the city was becoming less Irish, less Jewish, less Italian, and more black, Puerto Rican, and Latin American.

Chapter 8

Whither Ethnic America?
Assimilation into
American Life

THE massive flow of immigrants after the 1840s bewildered old-stock Americans. They could not agree on how the newcomers could best be absorbed into the mainstream of American life. The proponents of the melting pot had one theory, the Americanizers had another, and the advocates of pluralism had yet a third point of view. Americans eventually did agree upon one thing: Immigration must be restricted both in social composition and in numbers. Although they were willing to increase the numbers arriving after World War II and do away with the national origins systems, general restriction remained.

But what of the immigrants themselves? Did they and their descendants maintain separate subcultures, or did they blend with old Americans to form a new type, or did they assimilate into the larger society? As we have seen, the people who arrived in the colonial era eventually lost their distinct national heritages and became part of the common American culture. There are exceptions, of course, such as the Amish and Hutterites, who still live apart from the rest of society in their separate religious communities. But the Amish number only about 60,000 today, and the Hutterites are also few in number. Little remains now of the original Scotch-Irish, Welsh, German, or Huguenot societies of early America. The old immigrants, those coming in large numbers between 1840 and 1890 from northern and western Europe, have largely assimilated and lost much of their original culture. The new immigrants, coming after 1880 and now producing a fourth generation, have assimilated, although some Jews, Italians, Poles, and others still retain aspects of their traditional cultures. In fact, in the wake of the civil rights movement of the 1960s, there was a renewal of ethnic self-consciousness. Nevertheless, we believe that we are on the threshold of the disappearance of the European ethnic minorities. The most recent newcomers, especially the Spanish-speaking are, as we noted previously, still largely unassimilated. The United States Supreme Court's 1974 ruling in *Lau* v. *Nichols* which requires public schools to teach children in a language that they can understand, may inhibit the pace of future assimilation, or, paradoxically, it may hasten change by educating those who heretofore had been "turned off" by the schools.

The transition from foreign to American did not always come easily or without turmoil to those who made it. The German Americans, for example, who at the outbreak of World War I in Europe opposed American involvement on the side of the Allied powers against Germany, suffered severe anguish when the United States finally entered the conflagration in 1917. The issues were not clear-cut in spite of the shrill cries about German militarism, stories of atrocity, and the alleged threats to American interests. Moreover, when the United States entered the war against Germany, German Americans were faced with the reality of fighting against a nation in which many of their relatives and friends lived. Despite the acute agony caused by their situation, German-American soldiers fought as valorously as other Americans.

Yet American entry into the war forced all dissidents into an untenable position. The slightest indication of doubt or disagreement about the righteousness of the cause led to accusations of disloyalty and traitorous behavior. Superpatriots were especially critical of German Americans, the Irish, pacifists, and radicals. A few German Americans and some radicals such as Socialist party leader Eugene Debs continued to oppose the war once it came. Two sons of a prominent German Philadelphia brewing family, Erwin R. and Grover Cleveland Bergdoll, refused to serve because "we do not fight our own kind." One of the two was apprehended and sentenced to a federal prison while the other fled to Germany. Upon his return to the United States he too was imprisoned.

After the war some German Americans were bitter, but most accepted the war's outcome. When Hitler's armies marched in the 1930s, few German Americans supported him. American Nazi organizations in the 1930s, with small memberships, did have a few German immigrant members, but the second and third generations turned their backs on Nazism. Antiwar sentiments were vocal in German areas of the Midwest in the 1930s, but when World War II came, the descendants of German immigrants supported the United States without reservation.

The American Irish were also reluctant belligerents during World War I. Why, Irish-American leaders asked, should the Irish fight on the side of Great Britain when she had refused to free Ireland? It was a valid question, especially for Woodrow Wilson, a President who professed to make the war a crusade for democracy and the self-determination of nations. But the answer was relatively simple: As in the past one fought for his own country no matter what his personal preferences might be. Only a handful of Irish in America resisted the war effort, although others grumbled about the Allied powers. The omission of Irish independence from the peace treaty irked the Irish and caused some to desert the Democratic party; but these were political matters, hardly an issue of citizenship or disloyalty. Ireland achieved independence in 1926, before the coming of World War II. Thus the Irish question was largely dead, although some Irish were not overly sympathetic to Great Britain in the 1930s.

The crisis for Italian Americans, a new immigrant group, came later. Italian Americans had reservations about American foreign policy during the 1930s because of the growing friction between the United States and Italy. During the 1920s and 1930s, many Italian Americans and many other Americans admired Mussolini, but some bitterly opposed him and the advent of Fascism in Italy. The difficulty for the anti-Fascists was that they seemed to be "un-Italian" if they attacked Il Duce. An Italian American said: "Whatever you fellows may think of Mussolini, you've got to admit one thing: He has done more to get respect for the Italian people than anybody else. The Italians get a lot more respect now than when I started going to school. And you can thank Mussolini for that." The Italian attack on Ethiopia in 1935 aggravated the divisions. Some Italian Americans turned away from the Democratic party of Franklin Roosevelt, as some of the Irish had done over the question of Irish independence, because of Roosevelt's condemnation of Italy's actions.

The menace of Fascism and the coming of the war in Europe doomed such sentiments, however. Although many Italian Americans were uneasy about going to war against Italy, they supported the United States once war came. Even those segments of the Italian-American press that had praised Mussolini and Fascism in Italy proclaimed their loyalty to America and endorsed the American war effort.

The most excruciating test of loyalty faced by an ethnic group was that of Japanese Americans during World War II, which we discussed in Chapter 5. When the government interned the West Coast Japanese in 1942, no distinction was made between those who were citizens (Nisei) and their parents (Issei) who were born in Japan and ineligible for American citizenship. At first the army refused to draft the Nisei and did not allow them to enlist. The government insisted upon testing their patriotism further by making them answer a series of questions. The camp experience and the questionnaire divided many; a few Japanese were classified as disloyal to the United States and segregated at the Tule Lake, California, center. Several thousand of those classified as disloyal asked to be returned to Japan after the war, and some even renounced their American citizenship. Yet it was the familiar story. Most of the 110,000 interned Japanese Americans professed their allegiance to the United States and, when given the opportunity, the Nisei joined the army. About 33,000 Japanese Americans served, roughly half from the Hawaiian Islands and half from the mainland.

Since World War II there have been no major wars to divide ethnic attachments in America. Groups like the Irish and Italians do have strong loyalties either to Eire or Italy, but most of the immigrants' descendants have become too thoroughly Americanized to be as greatly troubled as their forebears had been during World War I. (The exception of the Jews and Israel will be discussed later.)

The longer that groups have lived in the United States, the more they have relinquished their Old World cultures. The first generation of immigrants retained their native languages or became bilingual. Their children and grandchildren gradually lost the old languages and spoke only English. Typically, when the United States government searched among second-generation Japanese

Americans in the camps during World War II for possible interpreters, it found that not many Nisei could speak and understand
Japanese well, and fewer still could read and write it. In 1974 a
middle-aged Czech woman noted the following about a declining
Czech community in New Jersey:

> The old Czechs are dying and moving away. Our parents are the
> ones who were very active. The people of my age still had their
> parents around. They remember the customs, and that is something
> you can't forget. But you can't pass memories on to your children.
> The younger generation marry people who are not Czech and don't
> keep up the language with their children. I go to see a friend of
> mine who's 83, and I talk Czech with her. If I didn't I'd forget
> the language.

Institutions depending upon foreign languages began to disappear as the immigrants' descendants could not use them. The Ger-
man-language press was thriving on the eve of World War I and
was the most important of the foreign-language presses; it accounted
for about 40 percent of the circulation of the foreign-language press.
The war shattered the German-American press and hurt the stand-
ing of the German language generally; it was driven off the news-
stands and out of the schools. In 1910 there were 70 German dailies
in America; in 1960 only 6 remained. Other major foreign-language
newspapers also declined, especially the Yiddish, Italian, and Scandinavian ones. Italian dailies decreased in number from 12 earlier
in the century to 5 in 1960; French dailies decreased in number
from 9 to 1 during the same period. From a high of 142 dailies in
1910 the foreign-language press has less than half that number
today, and the number and circulation of weeklies has dropped
about 75 percent in the same time. Of course, new immigrants from
Europe still read foreign-language newspapers, and in particular
isolated rural areas, such as in Minnesota or the Dakotas, they are
still important today. But in general, aside from those printed in
Spanish, the foreign-language press is declining in America.

The loss of the Old World culture can also be seen in the declining use of foreign languages in one of the most important immigrant institutions, the church. The Danish Lutheran churches are a
case in point. As the young learned English, the churches began to
abandon Danish. It was abandoned first in the Sunday schools in
the 1920s, then in youth work, and finally in the services a decade
later. Most of the books and periodicals published by Danish Lu-

therans in the late nineteenth century were in Danish, and as late as 1940 the annual reports for the United Evangelical Lutheran Church were about half in Danish, but the use of the language was discontinued after that.

The decline of foreign languages in churches was indicative of the growing Americanization and loss of ethnicity in American religion in the twentieth century. Lutheranism, which was originally divided mainly along ethnic or nationality lines such as Swedish, Danish, German, and Norwegian, is a good example of this process. In 1967 the United Evangelical Lutheran Church, of Danish background, merged with two other synods, one German and the other Norwegian in origin, and became the American Lutheran Church. Two years later another Danish Lutheran Church, the American Evangelical Lutheran Church, joined with German, Swedish, and Finnish synods to become the Lutheran Church in America. These various Lutheran groups were no longer using their old languages or recruiting ministers from the Old World, and since they already were cooperating in religious activities, they reached the inevitable conclusion: Merge into an American Lutheranism.

The same Americanization process happened in other denominations as well. In the late nineteenth century a burning issue in American Catholicism was the nationality parish supported ardently by, among others, German, French-Canadian, and Polish Catholics. The Church disapproved of nationality parishes in principle although it continued to allow them in practice. In the twentieth century, however, the nationality issue gradually became less important and so did the issue of national parishes.

The Germans are a case in point. In the 1890s German Catholics were most insistent upon having their own priests and organizations and fostered the slogan "Language Saves Faith." The largest of these organizations was the Central Verein, founded in 1855. It reached a peak membership of 125,000 on the eve of World War I and was especially strong in New York, Pennsylvania, and the Midwest. The second-generation German Catholics, however, were already losing interest in an ethnic church when the war began. Twenty-three German Catholic publications were discontinued between 1917 and 1923, and in those that remained English became prevalent during the 1920s. Membership in the Central Verein declined until it was 86,000 in 1930 and less than half of that a decade later. The journal of the Verein, *Central Blatt and Social Justice,* printed more of its material in English (it discontinued German sections entirely in 1946), changed its name to *Social Justice* in 1940, but still suffered a continued loss of interest; by the late 1960s circulation figures barely.exceeded 2,000.

As churches lost their national identities, so too did many of the other immigrant organizations. Social clubs, benefit societies, welfare organizations, and the like lost much of their membership and vitality as the old immigrant neighborhoods decayed. They are strongest today among those of new immigrant background, the Poles, and the Italians. The largest of the nationality organizations was the Deutsch-Amerikanische National Bund or National German-American Alliance, which was organized in 1901 to promote German culture in America and the interests of German Americans politically. At its peak before World War I it claimed a membership of about 2 million. In addition to promoting the German language and German culture, it was also an agent of assimilation, for it urged German immigrants to become citizens and insisted its primary loyalty was to the United States, not Germany. It opposed American entry on the side of England in World War I, came under attack during the war, and had to disband in 1918. It was not only the war that killed the Alliance, however; third-generation German Americans were not as interested in German culture as their parents and grandparents had been. In common with members of other minority groups they were moving out of the ethnic neighborhoods, especially after World War I, and joining assimilationist organizations.

Parents attempted to maintain the old ways through the use of ethnic or religious schools for their children. This was true of the Scandinavians, the Germans, the East European Jews, the Greeks, and the Chinese. Yet many of these schools have gradually dropped language teaching and have had difficulty attracting students. During the school crises of the 1960s and early 1970s, many parents did remove their children from the public schools to prevent racial integration, and as a result some of the ethnic schools, like the Jewish day schools, for example, did show a rise in the number of students; but it is questionable whether the main purpose was always devotion to the ancient heritage. The largest parochial school system in the United States is run by the Catholic Church. Only a minority of

Catholics attend these institutions despite the growth spurt in the 1950s and early 1960s. Financial troubles have beset the parochial schools, however, and since the late 1960s a number have had to close.

As the descendants of the immigrants improved their incomes, jobs, and education, they moved to the new neighborhoods in the cities and mushrooming suburbs. There they absorbed the values of the mass culture preached by the media and in the schools and came into social contact with a broad range of other people. These contacts led to growing intermarriage among different nationality and religious groups, the importance of which cannot be overstated. Family life is the primary social unit in society, and as families mix, so do other institutions. In other words, common intermarriage is the ultimate form of etl.nic assimilation.

For the first generation, on the contrary, intermarriage outside the ethnic group was rare. Many of the immigrants, who were disproportionately male, even returned to the mother land to find a spouse. Marriage within the group provided security and acceptance, outside of it disgrace and ostracism. When the children of orthodox Jews chose a Gentile mate, for example, their parents mourned for their children as though they had died. Roman Catholics were considered to be living in sin when they chose a Protestant spouse and married outside of the Catholic Church. Many states barred Orientals from marrying Caucasians. When individuals did venture outside their nationality group, however, they usually stayed within the same religious group, so that Irish Catholics married English or German Catholics (but rarely Italian Catholics!) and German Jews sometimes married East European Jews.

Data on intermarriage are not plentiful, but studies indicate that with assimilation the rates of intermarriage increase. One important study done of trends in New Haven, Connecticut, from 1870 to 1940, revealed that 91 percent married within the nationality group in 1870, 65 percent in 1930, and 63 percent in 1940. Thus the investigator found a decreasing tendency to marry within national groups but still a high tendency to marry within religious lines; in effect, national background faded while religion remained important. Eighty percent of the Protestants, 84 percent of the Catholics, and 94 percent of the Jews married within their respective faiths in 1940. The author drew the conclusion that instead of a single melting pot developing in American society, there was a triple melting pot—Protestant, Catholic, and Jewish groupings—and what intermarriage occurred happened within the three religious groups. Other scholars confirmed this as the direction of assimilation in America.

More recent data, though, suggest that the triple-melting-pot thesis is outdated. In Iowa, the only state that kept religious records in the 1950s, over 40 percent of the Jewish marriages were interfaith. A study of Jewish marriages in Washington, D.C., done in the 1960s, indicated that only 1 percent of the first but 10 percent of the second and 18 percent of the third generation married Gentiles. Alarmed by the growing rate of outmarriages among Jews, the Council for Jewish Federations and Welfare Funds conducted a national survey of the period 1966–1972. The results indicated that 31 percent of all Jews married during that period chose non-Jewish spouses.

Among Catholics in the 1960s about one in three married someone raised as a non-Catholic. The Irish and Germans were more apt to marry outside the nationality and religious group than the French Canadians, the Poles, or the Italians. Only about 40 percent of the Irish and Germans married other Irish or Germans during the 1960s, while the rate for Italians, Poles, and French Canadians was about 60 percent. Among the newest Catholic Americans from Mexico and Puerto Rico, early studies indicate that little intermarriage had taken place. Data for the 1960s and 1970s, though, shows an uptrend in their rates of intermarriage.

Recognizing the fact of increased intermarriage, the Roman Catholic Church modified some of its teachings in the mid-1960s. No longer were those who married outside the faith excommunicated. Non-Catholic clergy were also permitted to be present at a ceremony involving an interfaith marriage and to give a blessing after the exchange of vows. In 1973 an Eastern Rite Catholic professor of religious studies and pastor of a Ukrainian Catholic Church gave an opinion more sympathetic to the drift of public opinion: "The danger from increasing interfaith marriages is not that Catholics will join some other churches or religions—which would not be bad at all—but that they will become indifferent and estranged from religion in general." He concluded that "since the tide cannot be stemmed, it is useless to thunder from the pulpit against interfaith marriages. It would be more proficient if books were written and instruction provided so the partners with their children could practice both religions in meaningful, ecumenical understanding."

Among Protestants, despite variations, the trend has also been for increased incidence and acceptance of intermarriage. Among the Scandinavians, for example, the Swedes, like others, originally opposed marriage outside the group but were more apt to do so than the Norwegians. Most of the outmarriages of the Swedes occurred first with other Scandinavians or else with Germans, but those of the fourth generation have selected marriage partners from a wide assortment of different faiths and nationalities.

Recent polls indicate that a growing proportion of the American people accept interfaith marriage. In 1972, for example, the Gallup poll revealed that two-thirds of those asked approved of marriages between Protestants and Catholics; only 13 percent were opposed. The responses were even more favorable among the young and the well educated. A strong minority still resisted intermarriage, however. In 1974 Atlanta rabbis organized Jewish Compu-Date, a computer dating service for the city's widely dispersed Jewish singles. One rabbi explained its purpose: "We started Compu-Date . . . to preserve Judaism and our heritage; it is important that Jews meet and marry one another."

Interracial marriages between those of Oriental and European ancestry have also become more acceptable and common. Among Japanese Americans, for example, the intermarriage rates have soared. Largely prohibited by law and hostile custom, the Issei almost always married others of Japanese descent. Among the Nisei the rates of intermarriage rose, and by the late 1960s Japanese Americans were choosing marital partners having other backgrounds about half the time.

Several factors seem to influence the intermarriage rate. Persons who are well educated, mobile, and have good incomes are likely to intermarry. The culture and location of a group can also be important. The French Canadians, who have a relatively low intermarriage rate, are strongly nationalistic and are somewhat isolated in New England, near Canada; they travel easily back and forth across the Canadian-American border and thereby maintain their sense of identity more than most other groups do. But the most important variable for intermarriage seems to be time; the longer a group remains in the United States, the more it assimilates. As both the old and new immigrants are now moving beyond the third generation, one can expect to see increasing rates of intermarriage. Of course, not all interfaith marriages are losses to a particular group. Frequently, one partner converts, and the children are raised in that religion. It is too early to say, though, whether the children of these marriages will preserve the culture in which they are being reared.

Ethnic lines were becoming more blurred as the twentieth century progressed. The fall in immigration and drop in the number of foreign-born in America meant that the second and subsequent generations would have little contact with an Old World culture. The older immigrant institutions that had served the first generation were simply not as important to its descendants. There was, of course, a constant trickle of immigrants arriving in America to keep some old traditions alive, but it was of less significance than in the past because these immigrants sometimes no longer held on to the deeply rooted aspects of Old World culture.

The twentieth-century development of a public school system was certainly another key factor breaking down ethnicity. The immigrants' descendants were being instructed in Anglo-American values. After World War II most Americans attended and roughly three quarters graduated from the nation's high schools. In the post–World War II era colleges and universities rapidly expanded, and by the 1970s nearly one-half of the college-age population could be found in some institutions of higher learning. If elementary and high schools were often homogeneous, institutions of higher education were less so and exposed students to diverse ideologies and ethnic strains. Away from the watchful eyes of parents, the youth seemed more willing to learn about different people. No wonder ethnic leaders were concerned about intermarriage on college campuses!

Along with the expansion of education came the development of the mass media in American culture. The printed word was important before World War I in the form of the newspapers and journals, but after 1920 came the radio and movies and then, after World War II, television. Of course, many minorities did operate a press and run radio and TV stations, but they could not compete with the dominant corporations. The major networks possessed huge advertising budgets and national programs beamed identical messages into most American homes. Regardless of ethnic background, children were exposed to this mass culture of national products, common heroes, and similar values.

By and large, the descendants of the immigrants have absorbed this common culture. The traditional values of American society, originally propagated by the Puritans—like beliefs in success and individual achievement—have been accepted. National standards in dress and taste have also been observed. Musicians, movie stars, and athletes are almost universally acknowledged heroes and models. Even certain observances of religious holidays are becoming part of the national culture. A study of a Midwestern Jewish community done in the 1950s revealed that many Jewish families sent Christmas cards, exchanged gifts, and set up Christmas trees. We do not mean, of course, that all ethnic differences over values have disappeared and that Americans have become faceless mass men and women. We are suggesting, however, that the differences among peoples of different backgrounds have lessened and that peoples' values are often similar, if not homogenized.

The mobility of ethnic groups has also contributed to a loss of ethnicity. Businessmen and professionals, especially the more highly educated, have often joined organizations having mixed memberships. Upward mobility has also been accompanied by horizontal mobility, with large numbers of the descendants of immigrants moving out of the old neighborhoods and into the growing suburbs. In suburbia, where social divisions are often based on class and racial lines, it has been more difficult to maintain ethnicity. Common interests over local governmental questions such as education and zoning bring people together in a variety of activities.

The alleged religious revival that occurred after World War II, especially in the suburbs, was in part an attempt to create a bulwark of security in new surroundings. Church suppers and youth programs provided social entry for families until they could plant new roots. But the superficial religious revival of the 1950s was played out by the 1960s. More important was the development of new contacts among religious groups, which lead to increased toleration, which in turn opened new paths for social mobility and assimilation. Moreover, modern Judaism, Protestantism, and Catholicism have grown together ritually and theologically, thus further reducing differences and conflicts.

In the late 1960s, just when the European minorities seemed well on the way toward assimilation, ethnicity became a hot issue in

American life and politics. Cries for ethnic studies programs on college campuses, the proclamation of ethnic heritage days in cities, the formation of new ethnic organizations, and political assertions that the melting pot would not and should not work were all manifestations of this new interest in ethnicity. Not to be outdone, politicians, who have usually been aware of ethnic differences when courting votes, responded. In 1972 Congress, as part of the elementary and secondary education act, established an Ethnic Heritage Program and a National Advisory Council on Ethnic Heritage Studies. Funds were allocated to promote the study of the nation's ethnic heritage.

Among the ethnics themselves new groups appeared. Meir Kahane's Jewish Defense League (1968), although representing only a small minority of Jews, achieved headlines because of its demonstrations. Kahane lashed into the goal of assimilation and preached a militant brand of Jewish nationalism. Arrested for his activities in the United States, he went to Israel, where his militancy also brought him into confrontation with the law.

The Italians also showed a renewed concern with ethnicity. Joseph Columbo's Italian American Civil Rights League, founded in 1970, attacked alleged insults to Italian Americans and staged marches in New York City. Italian Americans vehemently protested the alleged prejudicial treatment that the media and law enforcement officials displayed. They resented, for example, television programs in which the underworld figure's name always ended with a vowel. They also railed against alleged discrimination by the Federal Bureau of Investigation (FBI) which they claimed unfairly portrayed Italian Americans as criminals. During the summer of 1971, groups of Italian Americans paraded in front of FBI headquarters in New York City chanting,

Hidi-hi
Hidi-ho
The FBI
Has got to go!

The new manifestations of ethnicity were sharp reminders that the process of Americanization was taking generations to achieve. Old groups like the Amish or new groups like the Hasidic Jews, who chose to remain in secluded enclaves, were at the far end of the spectrum of ethnicity in America. At the other end were the older groups that had been thoroughly blended into the Anglo-American culture; in between stood the descendants of the millions who came after 1880. The descendants of the new immigrants had lost much, probably most, of the Old World culture but still had some common bonds of religion, customs, political interest, and family and group life that held them together.

Social scientists are quick to remind us that ethnic voting behavior was and is important in American politics and often transcends class or regional lines. Politicians are clearly aware of ethnic trends in voting and regularly appear at the appropriate parades or eat pizza or bagels or chop suey. Orville Freeman, who served as governor of Minnesota and then as Secretary of Agriculture during the administrations of Presidents Kennedy and Johnson, attributed his defeat for reelection to the governorship in 1960 to the fact that his grandfather had changed the family name from Johnson, a name that strikes a responsive chord among the Scandinavians in Minnesota, to Freeman.

Ethnic politics is usually more intense at the city level, where political parties strive for ethnically balanced tickets. In New York City the three major elective posts—mayor, president of the city council and comptroller—have usually gone to people of Irish, Italian, and Jewish backgrounds when their votes were most significant. An Irish name is no longer politically significant, and politically the city's Italians seem to have moved toward the Republican or Conservative parties. Blacks and Puerto Ricans are now the ethnic groups, besides the Jews, to whom New York City Democrats are making appeals. In Buffalo a Polish name is an asset; in Milwaukee a German name is favored; and in parts of the Southwest a Hispanic name attracts votes.

The national political parties are also aware of the relationship between ethnic factors and voting. The Democrats had a temporary nationalities division in 1936 and made it permanent in 1948. As blacks, Poles, Italians, and Jews became more important to Democratic success, the party courted the ethnic vote more aggressively. John F. Kennedy brought Cleveland's Mayor Anthony Celebreeze into his cabinet as Secretary of Health, Education, and Welfare in 1962, and political pundits surmised that the President did so with one eye on the Italian vote. A year later the Democratic party made its newly named All American Council a more elaborate organization.

The Republican party responded more slowly to the new immigrant minorities, but in 1968 Richard Nixon made an attempt to capture votes from some of the white ethnic groups with promises and appeals to these people and appointments of their members to office. His final choice for a vice-presidential running mate was reputedly between John Volpe, of Italian background, and Spiro Agnew, of Greek ancestry. He chose the latter but placed the former in his cabinet as Secretary of Transportation. The Republicans also set up a nationalities division under the direction of Laszlo Pasztor, a Hungarian freedom fighter from the 1956 uprising. In 1971 the division, now called the National Republican Heritage Groups (Nationalities) Council, became a permanent part of the Republican party. Its goals before Watergate were "to attract the more than 40 million Americans of ethnic background to all levels of GOP activity; and to formalize the already substantial support among ethnic Americans for President Nixon's domestic and foreign policies."

To explain ethnicity it is important to reiterate the fact that each ethnic group has arrived in the United States with a unique life style. Roles of family members, expectations of spouses and children, and attitudes toward education and religion often determined how quickly and how well various minorities have been absorbed into American society. Members of those groups whose economic and educational aspirations were low and who therefore lacked mobility were least likely to be assimilated. Many Slavs, Italians, and members of the Spanish-speaking minorities would be included in this category. Unfortunately, for most people in the immigrant generation, the promises of American life remained unfulfilled. Their offspring, though, did have greater opportunities. By the 1960s militant members of the still depressed minorities demanded that the promises of American life become the realities—and quickly.

For this and other reasons there was a resurgence of ethnicity in the 1960s. The black civil rights and black nationalist movements emphasized a quest for identity, and some other ethnic groups sought to emulate black pressure-group tactics. Mexican Americans, Indians, and Italians were among the most prominent of the other ethnic groups that demonstrated for greater opportunities and respect in American society. They did not feel part of WASP America, and they wanted both recognition and celebration of their own backgrounds. The editor of a Polish-American weekly in New Jersey, for example, announced in 1970 the formation of "I'm Proud to be Polish" clubs.

The civil rights movements also sparked resentment among many whites who believed that the intellectuals, the government, and white elite groups (usually of old stock) were giving blacks favors at their expense. They did not share in the bounties of upper middle-class America, but they did have respect for the institutions of society and the traditional values of family solidarity, hard work, and patriotism. The severe inflation of the late 1960s and early 1970s aggravated their frustrations with ethnic as well as youthful protest groups of almost every variety, and they vented their anger against the most downtrodden minorities in society, especially the blacks. They wanted politicians to be tough with criminals, demonstrators, and rioters. They were especially concerned about busing their children into different neighborhoods to promote integrated schools. The movement sponsored by Alabama's Governor George Wallace appealed to this resentment as did the law-and-order campaign of Frank Rizzo for the mayoralty of Philadelphia in 1971. Rizzo concentrated his efforts in white working-class neighborhoods. A policeman by occupation, he said that he would not permit riots, marches, and demonstrations if he was elected. Perhaps the most acute form of this confrontation occurred in Newark, New Jersey, where a growing black population was pitted against a declining Italian hegemony led by Anthony Imperiale. Italian control of Newark was finally lost when Kenneth Gibson became the first black mayor elected in that city in 1970; he was reelected in 1974.

Not all white ethnic politics was a manifestation of white backlash. The Calumet Community Congress of Indiana, formed in 1970, tried to bring white ethnic groups and blacks together to deal with common problems. In Detroit, where many blacks and descendants of Poles lived, leaders of both groups organized the Black-Polish Conference in 1968 to work for their common interests. In 1971 the American Jewish Committee formed the National Project on Ethnic America to bridge the gap between whites and blacks. Its director said:

> We have a black problem and we have a white reaction to it. You can't solve the one without solving the other. Civil rights gains have been stalemated in many parts of the North and Midwest because the groups who are resisting have been left out. . . . The task is to push whites off a strictly negative anti-black agenda. We have to

make them conscious of their own realities. A new breed of ethnic leaders has to be developed who are as visible as the demagogues trying to exploit ethnic fears.

It was not the black movement alone that heightened ethnicity. The question of values in the 1960s also raised issues. Many descendants of the new immigrants had been ardent proponents of American nationalism as professions of their loyalty. They were especially hostile to the Soviet Union and her policies of oppression in eastern Europe. They were perplexed and confused by the war in Vietnam and the divisiveness that it prompted. Appeals to loyalty touched them and their conception of America. And when they came under attack, they were somewhat bitter about the sons and daughters of the affluent. In the confusion of the 1960s they, like so many other Americans, looked for security and a source of identity, and many found it in ethnicity. Ethnic identity was an answer for much of the alienation of the times.

Although ethnic and racial prejudice declined after the 1940s, it was not eradicated by the 1970s. It probably will never be eradicated until religious and racial intermarriage becomes more commonplace and one's ethnic background is of no more importance than the state in which one is born. The existence of prejudice serves as a reminder that many people are not fully accepted by the existing institutions and other Americans. This is turn reinforces minority reliance on a traditional heritage, for in the ethnic group one can find security. Churches, families, and social clubs fulfill this function, but organizations that combat prejudice are the best examples of ethnic loyalty. The Italian American Civil Rights League won a meaningless fight with Paramount Pictures to prevent the use of the word Mafia in the movie *The Godfather*. (Since the scriptwriters had never included the term anyway, the studio yielded quickly.) Other groups have pressured the Federal Communications Commission to eliminate offensive advertisements, programs, and movies from television screens. Japanese Americans objected to movies made during the early 1940s and their portrayal of the Japanese as virtual barbarians, while Mexican Americans blasted the Frito-Lay Company's "Frito Bandito" television commercials. In the summer of 1973 Puerto Rican pickets marched around the Gulf and Western Building in New York protesting the Paramount Pictures' film *Badge 373*. They charged that the film was racist because its villain was a Puerto Rican who dealt in prostitution and drugs.

One other aspect of ethnic associations remains to be covered—the concern with events in the home country. The civil war in Ireland does not have the impact in this country that earlier strife there aroused. Many of the Irish have married members of other groups and their descendants are too far removed from the old country to be more than sympathetic. The majority of Jews, on the other hand, although loyal and contented Americans, are deeply involved with the state of Israel. The creation of Israel in 1948 and the succession of conflicts with the Arabs in the Mideast, such as the Suez conflict of 1956, the Six-Day War of 1967, and the Yom Kippur War in 1973, drew lavish financial and moral support from Jews throughout the world. The emotional tie of American Jews to all other Jews, which is strengthened by the memory of past pogroms and the virtual genocide they faced in World War II, cannot be exaggerated. The Jews *feel* that Israel must survive and that all efforts must be made to ensure her survival. In addition to financial and moral support, therefore, American Jews have communicated their feelings to their political representatives in Washington.

These factors keep ethnicity alive and seem to blunt the pressures for complete Americanization and assimilation. It is hazardous to predict the future. Will religion remain important or will the nation become increasingly secular? Will national origins be the key issue? The forces undermining ethnicity—mass education, social mobility, and an American culture—are strong determinants that no group in the past has been able to withstand indefinitely. Our present estimate is that while resistance to assimilation might slow the pace of the Americanization process, it cannot prevent it. The latest descendants of the ethnic minorities appear eager to acquire good educations, find high-paying and satisfying jobs, and own beautiful homes in lovely neighborhoods. The goals of today's most vocal minority groups coincide with the demands of a majority of other Americans. Proponents for the retention of an ethnic way of life must ask what it can offer that would retard their children's absorption into the mainstream of American society when opportunities to do so present themselves. It does not appear likely today that any minority culture, except for small and dedicated groups like the Amish and Hutterites, can hold its own in the United States indefinitely.

Bibliographical Essay

THE best overall introduction to immigration history is Maldwyn Allen Jones, *American Immigration* (Chicago: University of Chicago Press, 1960). An older and somewhat biased factual account stressing the importance of those people who arrived before the twentieth century is Carl Wittke, *We Who Built America* (2nd ed., Cleveland: The Press of Western Reserve University, 1964). A penetrating analysis of the old immigration is Marcus Lee Hansen, *The Atlantic Migration, 1607–1860* (New York: Harper Torchbooks, 1961). Oscar Handlin's composite saga, *The Uprooted* (2nd ed., Boston: Little, Brown, 1973), is controversial and interpretive. Especially good for the European background is Philip Taylor, *The Distant Magnet* (New York: Harper & Row, 1971). A general collection of articles on ethnic groups is Leonard Dinnerstein and Frederic C. Jaher (eds.), *The Aliens: A History of Ethnic Minorities in America* (New York: Appleton-Century-Crofts, 1970), while a good documentary of white ethnics who arrived after 1830 is Stanley Feldstein and Lawrence Costello (eds.), *The Ordeal of Assimilation* (Garden City, N.Y.: Doubleday Anchor, 1974).

The literature on various immigrant and ethnic groups is enormous but of uneven quality. While some peoples have been the object of excellent scholarship, others have been neglected. The beginning reader might start with the following studies, most of which include bibliographic suggestions for those interested in penetrating the subject still further. James G. Leyburn, *The Scotch-Irish: A Social History* (Chapel

*Available in paperback

157

Hill: University of North Carolina Press, 1962) is a model monograph. John A. Hawgood, *The Tragedy of German-America* (New York: G. P. Putnam's Sons, 1940) and Richard O'Connor's anecdotal and breezy *The German-Americans* (Boston: Little, Brown, 1968) are good introductory books on the Germans. Arthur Henry Hirsch, *The Huguenots of Colonial South Carolina* (Durham: Duke University Press, 1928) is still the best single volume on the French Protestants in colonial America.

Oscar Handlin, *Boston's Immigrants* (revised and enlarged ed., New York: Atheneum, 1968) is an outstanding chronicle of the Irish of Boston. William Shannon, *The American Irish* (New York: Macmillan, 1963) is a general survey. Theodore Blegen, *Norwegian Migration to America* (Northfield, Minn.: Norwegian American Historical Association, 1940) is a first-rate analysis. Gunther Barth, *Bitter Strength: A History of the Chinese in the United States, 1850–1870* (Cambridge, Mass.: Harvard University Press, 1964) and Stanford M. Lyman, *Chinese Americans* (New York: Random House, 1974) treat the experiences of the Chinese in this country. On the Japanese Roger Daniels, *The Politics of Prejudice* (New York: Atheneum, 1968) and John Modell (ed.), *The Kikuchi Diary* (Urbana: The University of Illinois Press, 1973) are both worthwhile.

Italians have benefited within the past decade from renewed historical interest. Alexander De Conde, *Half Bitter, Half Sweet* (New York: Charles Scribner's Sons, 1971), Eric Amfitheatrof, *The Children of Columbus* (Boston: Little, Brown, 1973), and Richard Gambino, *Blood of My Blood* (New York: Doubleday and Company, 1974) are readable surveys, while Humbert Nelli, *The Italians of Chicago, 1880–1920* (New York: Oxford University Press, 1970) and Andrew F. Rolle, *The Immigrant Upraised* (Norman: University of Oklahoma Press, 1968) are regional histories of Italian Americans. *A Documentary History of the Italian Americans,* edited by Wayne Moquin and Charles Van Doren (New York: Praeger, 1974), has many revealing selections.

There is no satisfactory overall chronicle of the Jews in the United States, but Nathan Glazer, *American Judaism* (Chicago: University of Chicago Press, 1972) is the best. Moses Rischin, *The Promised City: New York's Jews, 1870–1914* (New York: Harper Torchbooks, 1970) and Arthur S. Goren, *New York Jews and the Quest for Community: The Kehillah Experiment: 1908–1922* (New York: Columbia University Press, 1970) are outstanding monographs. Leonard Dinnerstein, *The Leo Frank Case* (New York: Columbia University Press,

1968) deals with the single most violent outburst of anti-Semitism in American history, while Dinnerstein and Mary Dale Palsson (eds.), have collected many essays on *Jews in the South* (Baton Rouge: Louisiana State University Press, 1973). Theodore Saloutos, *The Greeks in the United States* (Cambridge, Mass.: Harvard University Press, 1964) is on a par with the best of the monographs, but Joseph A. Wytrwal, *America's Polish Heritage* (Detroit: Endurance Press, 1961) is not. Jacques Ducharme, *The Shadows of the Trees: The Story of the French-Canadians in New England* (New York: Harper and Brothers, 1943) is the best treatment we have on the French Canadians; new studies are needed. Many aspects of the history of the Swedes, Danes, Armenians, Slavs, and Chinese are still awaiting their chroniclers.

The easiest introduction to Mexican-American history is through two quite readable surveys: Carey McWilliams, *North from Mexico* (New York: Greenwood Press, 1968) and Matt S. Meier and Feliciano Rivera, *The Chicanos* (New York: Hill and Wang, 1972). Filipinos have not received adequate treatment. The most recent book on them is Alfred N. Munoz, *The Filipinos in America* (Los Angeles: Mountain View Publishers, 1971). Oscar Handlin, *The Newcomers: Negroes and Puerto Ricans in a Changing Metropolis* (New York: Doubleday Anchor Books, 1962) is the best historical work on the Puerto Ricans, but Joseph P. Fitzpatrick, *Puerto Rican Americans* (Englewood Cliffs, N.J.: Prentice-Hall, 1971) carries his analysis through the 1960s. On the Basques the reader might try William A. Douglass and Jon Bilbao, *Amerikanuak: The Basques in the New World* (Reno: University of Nevada Press, 1974). We know of no monograph that details the history of the Cubans in the United States since 1959.

For nativism and immigration restriction the standard work is John Higham, *Strangers in the Land: Patterns of American Nativism 1860–1925* (New York: Atheneum, 1963). For the early anti-immigrant crusade the reader should consult Ray Billington, *The Protestant Crusade 1800–1860* (Chicago: Quadrangle Press, 1964). An excellent account dealing with bigotry generally but also immigration restriction is Seymour Martin Lipset and Earl Raab, *The Politics of Unreason: Right-Wing Extremism in America 1790–1970* (New York: Harper & Row, 1970). Barbara Solomon, *Ancestors and Immigrants* (New York: John Wiley and Sons, 1965) is a probing study of the Immigration Restriction League. An older but still useful work about the immigration acts is Roy Garis, *Immigration Restriction* (New York: The Macmillan Company, 1928). More up to date is Marion T. Bennett,

American Immigration Policies: A History (Washington, D.C.: Public Affairs Press, 1963).

A great deal of information about ethnic mobility can be found in the works on various groups already noted. In addition, Niles Carpenter, *Immigrants and Their Children 1920* (Washington, D.C.: Government Printing Office, 1927) and Edward Hutchinson, *Immigrants and Their Children 1850–1950* (New York: John Wiley and Sons, 1956), both based on census data, are informative. Two books by Stephan Thernstrom are useful: *The Other Bostonians: Poverty and Progress in the American Metropolis 1880–1970* (Cambridge, Mass.: Harvard University Press, 1973) and **Poverty and Progress: Social Mobility in a 19th Century American City* (Cambridge, Mass.: Harvard University Press, 1964). Two penetrating analyses by Francis A. J. Ianni are **A Family Business Kinship and Social Control in Organized Crime* (New York: Russell Sage Foundation, 1972) and *Black Mafia: Ethnic Succession in Organized Crime* (New York: Simon and Schuster, 1974).

On the subject of assimilation Milton Gordon, **Assimilation in American Life: The Role of Race, Religion and National Origins* (New York: Oxford University Press, 1964) is a good beginning. Although Gordon's conclusions are open to criticism, his work is basic. Andrew Greeley, **Why Can't They Be Like Us?* (New York: E. P. Dutton, 1972) is lively and worth reading, as is Nathan Glazer and Daniel Moynihan, **Beyond the Melting Pot: The Negroes, Jews, Italians and Irish of New York City* (Cambridge, Mass.: The M.I.T. Press, 1963). Judith R. Kramer, *The American Minority Community* (New York: T. Y. Crowell, 1970) is less stimulating but rewarding. A profitable study on white Protestants is Charles Anderson, **White Protestant Americans: From National Origins to Religious Group* (Englewood Cliffs, N.J.: Prentice-Hall, 1970). Yonathan Shapiro, *Leadership of the American Zionist Organization 1897–1930* (Urbana: University of Illinois Press, 1971) is about the Jews; Harold J. Abramson, *Ethnic Diversity in Catholic America* (New York: John Wiley and Sons, 1973) is about the Catholics. Perry Wood, *The White Ethnic Movement and Ethnic Politics* (New York: Praeger Publications, 1973) is especially good on the recent ethnic revival. A provocative, but not totally convincing, argument against assimilation is presented by Michael Novak in **The Rise of the Unmeltable Ethnics* (New York: Macmillan, 1972).

Appendixes

Appendix I Immigration to the United States from Nation of Origin, 1820–1973[1]

[From 1820–1867, figures represent alien passengers arrived; from 1868–1891 and 1895–1897, immigrant aliens arrived; from 1892–1894 and 1898 to the present time, immigrant aliens admitted. Data for years prior to 1906 relates to country whence alien came; thereafter, to country of last permanent residence. Because of changes in boundaries and changes in lists of countries, data for certain countries is not comparable throughout.]

Countries	1820	1821–1830	1831–1840	1841–1850	1851–1860	1861–1870	1871–1880
All countries	8,385	143,439	599,125	1,713,251	2,598,214	2,314,824	2,812,191
Europe	7,690	98,797	495,681	1,597,442	2,452,577	2,065,141	2,271,925
Austria-Hungary[2][5]	—	—	—	—	—	7,800	72,969
Belgium	1	27	22	5,074	4,738	6,734	7,221
Denmark	20	169	1,063	539	3,749	17,094	31,771
France	371	8,497	45,575	77,262	76,358	35,986	72,206
Germany[2][5]	968	6,761	152,454	434,626	951,667	787,468	718,182
Great Britain:							
England	1,782	14,055	7,611	32,092	247,125	222,277	437,706
Scotland	268	2,912	2,667	3,712	38,331	38,769	87,564
Wales	—	170	185	1,261	6,319	4,313	6,631
Not specified[3]	360	7,942	65,347	229,979	132,199	341,537	16,142
Greece	—	20	49	16	31	72	210
Ireland	3,614	50,724	207,381	780,719	914,119	435,778	436,871
Italy	30	409	2,253	1,870	9,231	11,725	55,759
Netherlands	49	1,078	1,412	8,251	10,789	9,102	16,541
Norway[4] } Sweden[5] {	3	91	1,201	13,903	20,931	{ 71,631 / 37,667	{ 95,323 / 115,922
Poland[5]	5	16	369	105	1,164	2,027	12,970
Portugal	35	145	829	550	1,055	2,658	14,082
Romania[12]	—	—	—	—	—	—	11

Appendix I Immigration to the United States from Nation of Origin, 1820–1973[1] (Contd.)

Countries	1820	1821–1830	1831–1840	1841–1850	1851–1860	1861–1870	1871–1880
Spain	139	2,477	2,125	2,209	9,298	6,697	5,266
Switzerland	31	3,226	4,821	4,644	25,011	23,286	28,293
U.S.S.R.[5,6]	14	75	277	551	457	2,512	39,284
Other Europe	—	3	40	79	5	8	1,001
Asia	6	30	55	141	41,538	64,759	124,160
China	1	2	8	35	41,397	64,301	123,201
India	1	8	39	36	43	69	163
Japan[7]	—	—	—	—	—	186	149
Turkey	1	20	7	59	83	131	404
Other Asia	3	—	1	11	15	72	243
America	387	11,564	33,424	62,469	74,720	166,607	404,044
Canada & Newfoundland[8]	209	2,277	13,624	41,723	59,309	153,878	383,640
Mexico[9]	1	4,817	6,599	3,271	3,078	2,191	5,162
West Indies	164	3,834	12,301	13,528	10,660	9,046	13,957
Central America	2	105	44	368	449	95	157
South America	11	531	856	3,579	1,224	1,397	1,128
Africa	1	16	54	55	210	312	358
Australia & New Zealand	—	—	—	—	—	36	9,886
Pacific Islands (U.S. adm.)	—	—	—	—	—	—	1,028
Not specified	301	33,032	69,911	53,144	29,169	17,969	790

See footnotes at end of table.

SOURCE: Annual Report, U.S. Immigration and Naturalization Service, 1973.

163

Appendix I Immigration to the United States from Nation of Origin, 1820–1973[1] (Contd.)

Countries	1881–1890	1891–1900	1901–1910	1911–1920	1921–1930	1931–1940	1941–1950
All countries	5,246,613	3,687,564	8,795,386	5,735,811	4,107,209	528,431	1,035,039
Europe	4,735,484	3,555,352	8,056,040	4,321,887	2,463,194	347,552	621,124
Albania[11]	—	—	—	—	—	2,040	85
Austria }[2 5]	353,719	592,707	2,145,266	{453,649	32,868	3,563	24,860
Hungary }[2 5]				{442,693	30,680	7,861	3,469
Belgium	20,177	18,167	41,635	33,746	15,846	4,817	12,189
Bulgaria[10]	—	160	39,280	22,533	2,945	938	375
Czechoslovakia[11]	—	—	—	3,426	102,194	14,393	8,347
Denmark	88,132	50,231	65,285	41,983	32,430	2,559	5,393
Estonia	—	—	—	—	—	506	212
Finland[11]	—	—	—	756	16,691	2,146	2,503
France	50,464	30,770	73,379	61,897	49,610	12,623	38,809
Germany[2 5]	1,452,970	505,152	341,498	143,945	412,202	114,058	226,578
Great Britain:							
England	644,680	216,726	388,017	249,944	157,420	21,756	112,252
Scotland	149,869	44,188	120,469	78,357	159,781	6,887	16,131
Wales	12,640	10,557	17,464	13,107	13,012	735	3,209
Not specified[3]	168	67	—	—	—	—	—
Greece	2,308	15,979	167,519	184,201	51,084	9,119	8,973
Ireland	655,482	388,416	339,065	146,181	220,591	13,167	26,967
Italy	307,309	651,893	2,045,877	1,109,524	455,315	68,028	57,661
Latvia[11]	—	—	—	—	—	1,192	361
Lithuania[11]	—	—	—	—	—	2,201	683
Luxembourg[15]	—	—	—	—	—	565	820
Netherlands	53,701	26,758	48,262	43,718	26,948	7,150	14,860
Norway[4]	176,586	95,015	190,505	66,395	68,531	4,740	10,100
Poland[5]	51,806	96,720	—	4,813	227,734	17,026	7,571

Appendix I Immigration to the United States from Nation of Origin, 1820–1973[1] (Contd.)

Countries	1881–1890	1891–1900	1901–1910	1911–1920	1921–1930	1931–1940	1941–1950
Portugal	16,978	27,508	69,149	89,732	29,994	3,329	7,423
Romania[12]	6,348	12,750	53,008	13,311	67,646	3,871	1,076
Spain	4,419	8,731	27,935	68,611	28,958	3,258	2,898
Sweden[4]	391,776	226,266	249,534	95,074	97,249	3,960	10,665
Switzerland	81,988	31,179	34,922	23,091	29,676	5,512	10,547
U.S.S.R.[5,6]	213,282	505,290	1,597,306	921,201	61,742	1,356	548
Yugoslavia[10]	—	—	—	1,888	49,064	5,835	1,576
Other Europe	682	122	665	8,111	22,983	2,361	3,983
Asia	69,942	74,862	323,543	247,236	112,059	16,081	32,360
China	61,711	14,799	20,605	21,278	29,907	4,928	16,709
India	269	68	4,713	2,082	1,886	496	1,761
Japan[7]	2,270	25,942	129,797	83,837	33,462	1,948	1,555
Turkey	3,782	30,425	157,369	134,066	33,824	1,065	798
Other Asia	1,910	3,628	11,059	5,973	12,980	7,644	11,537
America	426,967	38,972	361,888	1,143,671	1,516,716	160,037	354,804
Canada & Newfoundland[8]	393,304	3,311	179,226	742,185	924,515	108,527	171,718
Mexico[9]	1,913	971	49,642	219,004	459,287	22,319	60,589
West Indies	29,042	33,066	107,548	123,424	74,899	15,502	49,725
Central America	404	549	8,192	17,159	15,769	5,861	21,665
South America	2,304	1,075	17,280	41,899	42,215	7,803	21,831
Other America[13]	—	—	—	—	31	25	29,276
Africa	857	350	7,368	8,443	6,286	1,750	7,367
Australia & New Zealand	7,017	2,740	11,975	12,348	8,299	2,231	13,805
Pacific Islands (U.S. adm.)	5,557	1,225	1,049	1,079	427	780	5,437
Not specified[14]	789	14,063	33,523	1,147	228	—	142

See footnotes at end of table.

Appendix I Immigration to the United States from Nation of Origin, 1820–1973[1] (Contd.)

Countries	1951–1960	1961–1965	1966	1967	1968
All countries	2,515,479	1,450,312	323,040	361,972	454,448
Europe	1,325,640	528,543	115,319	128,098	128,396
Albania[11]	59	48	10	15	9
Austria[2][6]	67,106	6,638	1,446	1,484	2,022
Hungary[2][6]	36,637	2,591	629	582	534
Belgium	18,575	5,463	887	862	754
Bulgaria[10]	104	397	57	43	43
Czechoslovakia[11]	918	1,005	286	297	398
Denmark	10,984	4,987	953	991	1,126
Estonia[11]	185	94	23	17	11
Finland[11]	4,925	2,164	356	449	586
France	51,121	24,431	4,184	4,904	4,815
Germany[2][6]	477,765	118,945	17,654	16,595	16,590
Great Britain:					
England	156,171	88,730	16,020	20,257	22,970
Scotland	32,854	19,489	2,573	2,552	2,818
Wales	2,589	1,167	184	195	237
Not specified[3]	3,884	696	664	774	727
Greece	47,608	19,290	8,236	14,194	12,185
Ireland	57,332	27,844	2,603	1,991	2,268
Italy	185,491	78,893	26,447	28,487	25,882
Latvia[11]	352	261	67	62	37
Lithuania[11]	242	344	63	49	48
Luxembourg[15]	684	303	59	50	66
Netherlands	52,277	22,218	1,924	1,786	2,051
Norway[4]	22,935	10,301	1,599	1,282	1,196

Appendix I Immigration to the United States from Nation of Origin, 1820–1973[1] (Contd.)

Countries	1951–1960	1961–1965	1966	1967	1968
Poland[5]	9,985	32,889	8,490	4,356	3,676
Portugal	19,588	14,308	8,482	13,400	11,827
Romania[12]	1,039	1,158	242	179	214
Spain	7,894	16,057	4,944	4,562	7,904
Sweden[4]	21,697	10,095	1,863	1,822	1,748
Switzerland	17,675	9,921	1,995	2,279	2,187
U.S.S.R.[5 6]	584	872	259	299	292
Yugoslavia[10]	8,225	5,395	1,611	2,753	2,705
Other Europe	8,155	1,549	509	530	470
Asia[16]	150,106	107,032	40,692	58,251	56,924
China[17]	9,657	8,156	2,948	7,118	4,851
India	1,973	2,602	2,293	4,129	4,165
Japan[7]	46,250	19,759	3,468	4,125	3,810
Turkey	3,519	4,330	944	1,168	951
Other Asia	88,707	72,185	31,039	41,711	43,147
America	996,944	795,080	162,551	170,235	262,736
Canada & Newfoundland[8]	377,952	243,400	37,273	34,768	41,716
Mexico[9]	299,811	228,401	47,217	43,034	44,716
West Indies	123,091	119,596	37,999	61,987	140,827
Central America	44,751	52,182	9,889	8,862	11,051
South America	91,628	138,052	28,113	18,562	23,991
Other America[13]	59,711	13,449	2,060	3,022	435
Africa	14,092	9,631	1,967	2,577	3,220
Australia & New Zealand	11,506	8,195	1,894	2,128	2,374
Pacific Islands (U.S. adm.)[16]	4,698	848	177	149	139
Not specified[14]	12,493	983	440	534	659

See footnotes at end of table.

Appendix I Immigration to the United States from Nation of Origin, 1820–1973[1] (Contd.)

Countries	1969	1970	1971	1972	1973	Total 154 years 1820–1973
All countries	358,579	373,326	370,478	384,685	400,063	46,317,864
Europe	113,198	109,809	91,509	86,321	91,183	35,807,902
Albania[11]	9	7	4	8	99	2,393
Austria[2 5]	3,762	5,269	1,945	2,251	1,589 }	4,309,625
Hungary[2 5]	517	548	488	475	1,008 }	
Belgium	562	664	577	530	438	199,706
Bulgaria[10]	38	41	44	40	212	67,250
Czechoslovakia[11]	532	755	734	1,152	910	135,347
Denmark	580	564	492	503	439	362,037
Estonia[11]	8	10	5	12	10	1,093
Finland[11]	247	390	331	341	283	32,168
France	3,203	3,700	2,844	2,870	2,587	738,466
Germany[2 5]	10,380	10,632	8,646	7,760	7,565	6,941,061
Great Britain:						
England	13,522	12,953	11,125	10,036	10,450	3,115,677
Scotland	1,397	1,020	740	947	790	815,085
Wales	153	116	62	85	99	94,490
Not specified[3]	419	395	375	453	521	802,649
Greece	16,634	15,430	15,002	10,452	10,349	608,960
Ireland	1,567	1,188	1,173	1,423	1,588	4,718,052
Italy	27,033	27,369	22,818	22,413	22,264	5,243,981
Latvia[11]	38	45	27	28	14	2,484
Lithuania[11]	27	31	20	25	18	3,751
Luxembourg[15]	35	43	46	26	26	2,723

Appendix I Immigration to the United States from Nation of Origin, 1820-1973[1] (Contd.)

Countries	1969	1970	1971	1972	1973	Total 154 years 1820–1973
Netherlands	1,285	1,342	1,092	979	966	354,539
Norway[4]	602	504	409	375	394	854,552
Poland[5]	2,115	2,013	1,928	3,770	4,136	495,684
Portugal	15,785	12,263	10,545	9,465	10,019	389,149
Romania[12]	266	472	687	354	1,106	163,738
Spain	5,929	5,263	3,661	4,284	5,538	239,057
Sweden[4]	789	799	648	654	597	1,268,825
Switzerland	859	1,212	1,066	999	704	345,124
U.S.S.R.[5][6]	254	360	303	400	874	3,348,392
Yugoslavia[10]	4,078	3,839	3,265	2,767	5,213	98,214
Other Europe	573	572	407	444	378	53,630
Asia[16]	73,813	91,059	98,062	115,978	119,984	2,018,673
China[17]	5,264	6,427	7,597	8,511	9,153	468,564
India	5,205	8,795	13,056	15,589	11,975	81,416
Japan[7]	4,095	4,731	4,649	5,037	6,104	381,174
Turkey	1,410	1,339	1,147	1,531	1,447	379,820
Other Asia	57,839	69,767	71,613	85,310	91,305	707,699
America	164,045	161,727	171,680	173,165	179,604	7,994,037
Canada & Newfoundland[8]	29,303	26,850	22,709	18,596	14,800	4,024,813
Mexico[9]	45,748	44,821	50,324	64,209	70,411	1,777,536
West Indies	53,190	56,614	66,552	60,386	62,830	1,279,768

See footnotes at end of table.

Appendix I Immigration to the United States from Nation of Origin, 1820–1973¹ (Contd.)

Countries	1969	1970	1971	1972	1973	Total 154 years 1820–1973
Central America	9,857	9,489	8,870	8,407	9,125	243,302
South America	25,542	23,694	22,678	21,393	22,423	559,209
Other America¹³	405	259	547	174	15	109,409
Africa	4,460	7,099	5,844	5,472	5,537	93,326
Australia & New Zealand	2,278	2,693	2,357	2,550	2,466	106,778
Pacific Islands (U.S. adm.)¹⁶	225	231	158	235	176	23,618
Not specified¹⁴	560	708	868	964	1,113	273,530

¹ Since July 1, 1868, the data is for fiscal years ending June 30. Prior to fiscal year 1869, the periods covered are as follows: from 1820–1831 and 1843–1849, the years ended on September 30—1843 covers 9 months; and from 1832–1842 and 1850–1867, the years ended on December 31—1832 and 1850 cover 15 months. For 1868, the period ended on June 30 and covers 6 months.

² Data for Austria-Hungary was not reported until 1861. Austria and Hungary have been recorded separately since 1905. From 1938–1945, Austria is included in Germany.

³ Great Britain not specified. From 1901–1951, included in other Europe.

⁴ From 1820–1868, the figures for Norway and Sweden are combined.

⁵ Poland recorded as a separate country from 1820–1898 and since 1920. From 1899–1919, Poland is included with Austria-Hungary, Germany, and Russia.

⁶ From 1931–1963, the U.S.S.R. is broken down into European U.S.S.R. and Asian U.S.S.R. Since 1964 total U.S.S.R. has been reported in Europe.

⁷ No record of immigration from Japan until 1861.

⁸ Prior to 1920, Canada and Newfoundland are recorded as British North America. From 1820–1898, the figures include all British North American possessions.

⁹ No record of immigration from Mexico from 1886–1893.

[10] Bulgaria, Serbia, and Montenegro were first reported in 1899. Bulgaria has been reported separately since 1920; also in 1920, a separate enumeration was made for the Kingdom of Serbs, Croats, and Slovenes. Since 1922, the Serbs, Croat, and Slovene Kingdom has been recorded as Yugoslavia.

[11] Countries added to the list since the beginning of World War I are included with the countries to which they belonged. Figures available since 1920 for Czechoslovakia and Finland and, since 1924, for Albania, Estonia, Latvia, and Lithuania.

[12] No record of immigration from Romania until 1880.

[13] Included with countries not specified to 1925.

[14] The figure 33,523 in column headed 1901–1910 includes 32,897 persons returning in 1906 to their homes in the United States.

[15] Figures for Luxembourg are available since 1925.

[16] Beginning with the year 1952, Asia includes the Philippines. From 1934–1951, the Philippines are included in the Pacific Islands. Prior to 1934, the Philippines are recorded in separate tables as insular travel.

[17] Beginning with the year 1957, China includes Taiwan.

171

Appendix II   Jewish Immigration to the United States, 1899–1973

Fiscal Years*	ABSOLUTE NUMBERS		Percentage of Jewish Immigrants
	Jews	Total	
1899	37,415	311,715	12.0
1900	60,764	448,572	13.5
1901	58,098	487,918	11.9
1902	57,688	648,743	8.9
1903	76,203	857,046	8.9
1904	106,236	812,870	13.1
1905	129,910	1,026,499	12.7
1906	153,748	1,100,735	14.0
1907	149,182	1,285,349	11.6
1908	103,387	782,870	13.2
1909	57,551	751,786	7.7
1910	84,260	1,041,570	8.1
1911	91,223	878,587	10.4
1912	80,595	838,172	9.6
1913	101,330	1,197,892	8.5
1914	138,051	1,218,480	11.3
1915	26,497	326,700	8.1
1916	15,108	298,826	5.1
1917	17,342	295,403	5.9
1918	3,672	110,618	3.3
1919	3,055	141,132	2.2
1920	14,292	430,001	3.3
1921	119,036	805,228	14.8
1922	53,524	309,556	17.3
1923	49,719	522,919	9.5
1924	49,989	706,896	7.1
1925	10,292	294,314	3.5
1926	10,267	304,488	3.4
1927	11,483	335,175	3.4
1928	11,639	307,255	3.8
1929	12,479	279,678	4.5
1930	11,526	241,700	4.8
1931	5,692	97,139	5.9
1932	2,755	35,576	7.7
1933	2,372	23,068	10.3

SOURCES: *Jewish People: Past and Present*, Vol. I, p. 407. Published by Jewish Encyclopedia Handbooks, Inc., 1946; *American Jewish Yearbook;* and United Hebrew Immigrant Aid Society.

Appendix II   Jewish Immigration to the United States, 1899–1973 (Contd.)

| Fiscal Years* | ABSOLUTE NUMBERS | | Percentage of Jewish Immigrants |
	Jews	Total	
1934	4,134	29,470	14.0
1935	4,837	34,956	13.8
1936	6,252	36,329	17.2
1937	11,352	50,244	22.6
1938	19,736	67,895	29.0
1939	43,450	82,998	52.3
1940	36,945	70,756	52.2
1941	23,737	51,776	45.8
1942	10,608	28,781	36.9
1943	4,705	23,725	19.8
1944	2,400	28,551	8.4
1945	4,160	38,119	10.9
1946	12,774	108,721	11.8
1947	29,274	147,292	19.9
1948	17,581	170,570	10.3
1949	41,222	188,317	21.9
1950	13,057	249,187	5.2
1951	18,239	205,717	8.8
1952	7,800	265,520	2.9
1953	5,353	170,434	3.1
1954	3,933	208,177	1.9
1955	3,253	237,790	1.4
1956	6,513	321,625	2.0
1957	10,876	326,867	3.3
1958	7,160	253,265	2.8
1959	8,098	260,686	3.1
1960	6,622	265,398	2.5
1961	7,102	271,344	2.6
1962	9,325	283,763	3.3
1963	10,750	306,260	3.3
1964	9,300	292,248	3.2
1965	7,800	296,697	2.6
1966	7,500	323,040	2.3
1967	6,600	361,972	1.8
1968	7,800	454,448	1.7
1969	9,300	358,579	2.6
1970	7,700	373,326	2.1

* From July 1st of the preceding year to June 30th of the year stated.

Appendix II   Jewish Immigration to the United States, 1899–1973 (Contd.)

| Fiscal Years* | ABSOLUTE NUMBERS | | Percentage of Jewish Immigrants |
	Jews	Total	
1971	5,525	370,478	1.5
1972	5,520	384,685	1.5
1973	6,625	400,063	1.6
Totals 1899–1973	2,381,298	27,954,545	8.5

* From July 1st of the preceeding year to June 30th of the year stated.

Appendix III

Ethnic Background of the American Population, 1971

RACE AND ETHNIC ORIGIN	TOTAL
Total	202,848,000
Race	
White	177,626,000
Negro	22,810,000
Other races	2,412,000
Ethnic Origin	
English, Scotch, Welsh	31,006,000
French	5,189,000
German	25,661,000
Irish	16,325,000
Italian	8,733,000
Polish	4,941,000
Russian	2,132,000
Spanish origin	8,956,000
Central or South American	501,000
Cuban	626,000
Mexican	5,023,000
Puerto Rican	1,450,000
Other Spanish origin	1,356,000
Other ethnic origin†	84,689,000
Not reported	15,216,000

† Includes about 20 million Negroes, as well as many persons reporting more than one origin.

SOURCE: U.S. Bureau of the Census, "Selected Characteristics of Persons and Families of Mexican, Puerto Rican and other Spanish Origin: March 1971," Series P-20, No. 224, October 1971, Table 1.

Appendix IV

Provisions of the Major United States Immigration Laws and Programs

(1) 1819   The Federal government requires numeration of immigrants.

(2) 1864   Congress passes a law facilitating the importation of contract laborers.

(3) 1875   Congress passes the first federal restriction of immigration, prohibiting the importation of prostitutes and alien convicts.

(4) 1882   The Chinese Exclusion Act curbs the immigration of the Chinese.

(5) 1882   Congress excludes convicts, lunatics, idiots, or persons likely to become a public charge and places a head tax on immigration.

(6) 1885   The contract labor laws end.

(7) 1891   The federal government assumes the supervision of immigration and the next year opens Ellis Island.

(8) 1903   Congress expands the list of excluded immigrants to include polygamists, anarchists, and other radicals.

(9) 1907   Congress raises the head tax on immigrants and adds to the excluded list persons with physical or mental defects which might affect their ability to earn a living, those with tuberculosis, and children unaccompanied by their parents.

(10) 1907   The United States and Japan agree to the Gentlemen's Agreement restricting immigration from Japan.

(11) 1917   Congress codifies previously excluded classes and includes a literacy test banning those over 16 who could not read some language. Persons escaping from religious persecution were exempt from the literacy test. The law also banned virtually all immigration from Asia.

(12) 1921   Congress sets a limit on European immigration of approximately 358,000. National quotas were instituted and based on a formula allowing each nation 3% of foreign-born persons of that nationality who lived here in 1910.

(13) 1924   Congress enacts the Johnson-Reed Act. This act set the annual quota of any nationality at 2% of the number of foreign-born of each nationality resident in the United States according to the 1890 census. This quota was replaced in 1927 with the national origins provision. Under the national origins provision each nationality was permitted a quota based on its proportion of the population according to the 1920 census. Proportions were based on a figure of 153,714 annually from Europe.

(14) 1924 The Oriental Exclusion Act bans immigration from Asia.

(15) 1930 President Herbert Hoover directs consuls to enforce strictly the provisions of the immigration acts barring "those likely to become a public charge."

(16) 1942 The United States and Mexico agree to the Bracero program permitting temporary foreign laborers to work in the United States.

(17) 1943 Congress repeals the ban on Chinese immigration.

(18) 1946 Congress passes the War Brides Act facilitating the entry of alien wives, husbands, and children of members of the United States armed forces.

(19) 1948 Congress enacts the Displaced Persons Act allowing the entrance of displaced persons in addition to those admitted under the annual quotas.

(20) 1952 Congress passes the McCarren-Walter Immigration and Naturalization Act. It
—eliminated race as a bar to immigration and naturalization.
—reaffirmed the national origins system but gave every nation a quota.
—provided for a more thorough screening of immigrants.
—established preferences for those who had relatives in America or those who had skills.

(21) 1953 Congress enacts the Refugee Relief Act authorizing the admission of special nonquota refugees.

(22) 1957 Congress passes the Refugee-Escape Act liberalizing the McCarren-Walter Act by allowing more nonquota immigrants to enter.

(23) 1960 Congress passes the World Refugee Year Law permitting the entrance of additional refugees.

(24) 1964 The United States and Mexico terminate the Bracero program.

(25) 1965 Congress passes the Immigration Act of 1965. The act
—abolished the national origins system.
—established a limit of 170,000 outside the Western Hemisphere but placed a limit of 20,000 on any one country. Immigrants were to be received on a first come first qualified basis.
—established preferences for close relatives as well as those who had occupational skills needed in the United States.
—placed a ceiling of 120,000 on immigration from the Western Hemisphere.

Index

179